Kilim Designs
in Needlepoint

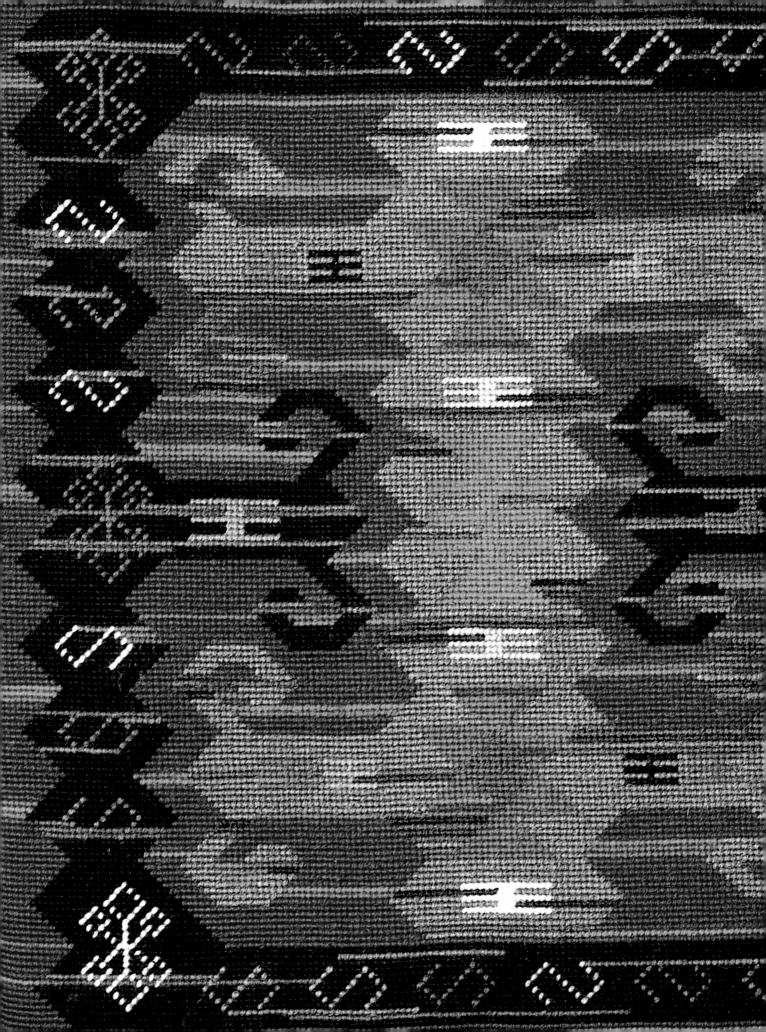

Kilim Designs in Needlepoint

Over 25 Projects Inspired by Traditional Kilim Patterns

....

Dorothy Wood

WARD LOCK

For my sister, Linda

A WARD LOCK BOOK

First published in the UK 1998 by
Ward Lock
Wellington House
125 Strand
London WC2R 0BB

A Cassell Imprint

Distributed in the United States by
Sterling Publishing Co. Inc.
387 Park Avenue South
New York NY 10016-8810
USA

British Library Cataloguing-in-Publication Data
A catalogue record for this book is available from the British Library

Edited by Vivienne Wells

Designed by Gail Engert

Photography by Ed Barber, except for photographs on pages 7, 8 and 9
© The Kilim Warehouse Ltd, 28a Pickets Street, London SW12 8QB
(Tel: 0181 675 3122)

Illustrations by Kate Simunek

ISBN 0-7063-7727-3

Colour separations by Reed Digital, Ipswich, Suffolk.
Printed and bound by South China Printing Co. Ltd, Hong Kong / China

Many readers find it easier to stitch from an enlarged photocopy
of a chart. The publishers are happy to allow this use provided
the photocopies are for personal use only.

BF-16-99

CONTENTS

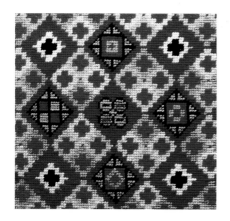

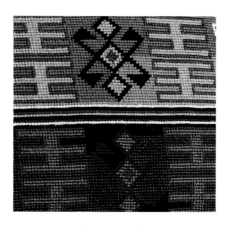

Introduction

....

The needlepoint designs in this book are inspired by the bold, brilliantly-patterned, woven kilims of the people of central Asia. Even in our era of mass production and manufactured materials, the kilim tradition of weaving still uses ancient skills passed down through generations. The colourful rugs and covers known as kilims are woven by families and peoples working together to collect the raw materials, then spin, dye and weave the wool. Each ethnic group, village, or even family, has its own distinctive motifs and colour combinations, so there is an enormous variation of colour and pattern throughout the extensive area where kilims are made.

The designs are based on kilims from the three main areas of kilim production: Afghanistan, Anatolia (Turkey) and Persia (Iran). There is a wide variety of projects, though this selection represents only a fraction of the kilim designs that are available for inspiration. All projects are stitched entirely in tent stitch on canvas. There are larger projects such as rugs, wallhangings and cushions, and many smaller projects, such as bags, and even a hat! The small projects make ideal gifts.

I do hope that you enjoy looking through the book and choosing your first project to stitch. Whether you are experienced or just beginning, there is plenty of choice, because the geometric style of kilim design ensures that every project is easy to stitch. When making up, the needlepoint kilims can be finished simply, or adorned with tassels and fringes in the traditional tribal fashion.

Full instructions for all techniques are given at the back of the book. Before beginning any project, it is a good idea to read through 'Materials and Equipment' and 'Techniques'.

KILIMS

....

The majority of peoples in central Asia, from rural nomads to settled farmers, are united by Islam. This provides a structured, conservative framework that has inspired a wealth of sophisticated motifs and patterns. Each ethnic group retains its identity by using particular symbols, patterns and colours.

True nomads live in tents (yurts) all year round, migrating with their livestock between summer and winter grazing. Semi-nomadic people live part of the year in

Kilim in the traditional
Maimana style from northern
Afghanistan, with a reciprocal
hook design in the borders
and main field

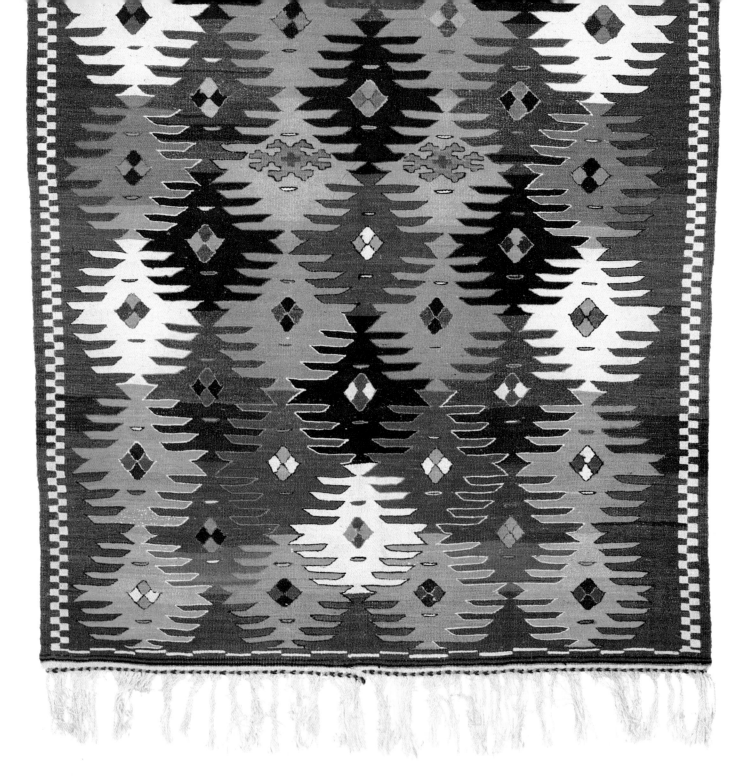

villages, and part in tents. Kilims traditionally play an important part in local life, whether it is nomadic or settled. Woven to provide functional and decorative rugs, bags and accoutrements for homes and animals, the best kilims are given as gifts, or are used only when guests arrive, or for special occasions, such as weddings.

Nomads have traditionally relied on natural resources to make their kilims. Using basic portable looms built from tree branches, and wool from their flocks, dyed with natural materials, they have produced a remarkable range of stunning rugs. Using just six basic ingredients (oak galls, madder root, indigo, yellow dye plant, alum and iron sulphate), the dyer was able to produce the typical kilim colour palette of between six and thirteen colours. Indigo blue, madder red, yellow and

Unusual and powerful design from Konya in Anatolia, featuring interlocking parmakli or finger motifs

oak-gall black can be combined to produce several blues and reds, as well as apricot, purple, orange, yellow, green, black and natural white. The combination of colours used in the kilim is very much up to the individual, but the palette is determined by local traditions and the skill of the dye specialist.

After the introduction of aniline dyes in the late-nineteenth century, many of the traditional dye recipes were forgotten. Weavers liked the bright colours of the synthetic dyes, so they stopped using natural dyes. Unfortunately for the weavers, the new, brighter kilims were unpopular in the West, so they had to be sun-bleached to make them saleable to western markets. In recent years, kilims

Shahsavan kilim woven in a band format, with typical eight-pointed stars

woven by remote nomadic peoples have appeared on the market from time to time, sparking an interest in, and demand for, naturally-dyed kilims. Projects have been set up in Turkey, Iran and Afghanistan to re-introduce the complex process of vegetable dying.

One of the endearing qualities of kilims is the existence of imperfections in colour, which are more pronounced on kilims whose yarns have been hand spun and dyed using vegetable dyes. The innumerable variations of the same shade in one block of colour are known as abrash. There are two types of abrash. One is brought about by uneven spinning. Thicker parts of the wool absorb more dye and appear darker, giving the weaving a mottled overall appearance. The other type of abrash is a horizontal colour change that occurs when changing from one dye batch to another (exact matches in natural dyes are almost impossible to produce). Abrash gives vitality and life to flat areas of colour in the kilim.

Despite a degree of commercialism seeping into kilim production, kilims are still, on the whole, handmade products, intended for personal use. Unlike commercial rugs which have no individuality, each kilim is different. Even if the colours and pattern are copied, the variations in hand-spun wool, natural dyes and local weaving techniques make each kilim unique.

Parmakli

MOTIFS, PATTERNS AND SYMBOLISM
....

Traditionally, the weaving of kilims is the women's domain. Girls learn to weave on tiny toy looms. Once competent, they begin to help their mothers or grandmothers on full-size kilims before working on their own. Girls are betrothed at an early age, and they are obliged to produce a dowry of quality and quantity, to include kilims.

Kilims are often woven from memory. Children 'absorb' the patterns, in the same way they pick up language, and, from an early age, they give the patterns nicknames such as 'arrow', 'mouse tail' and 'comb'. The symbolism attached to individual motifs is passed down through the generations by word

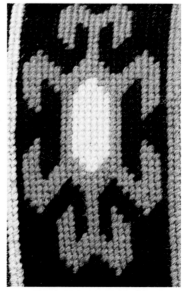

Koçboynuzu

Yildiz

Göz

Nazarlik

of mouth and oral storytelling traditions. The original meaning will have been amended and embroidered over time, as the symbolism became part of folklore (and as market traders exaggerated stories to help sell their products).

Kilims are a form of visual communication, expressing the weaver's hopes for continued good fortune, fertility and protection from evil spirits. The frequently abstract symbols are sometimes incorporated in a repeat motif, or scattered randomly over the 'field', the background of the main area inside the border.

There is not necessarily a meaning for every motif or pattern found in kilims, but the following are well documented: Parmakli are comb-like protrusions from motifs and borders, said to represent the hand of Mother Fatima. This suggests the

Çengel

desire to be married and offers protection to a couple and their offspring. The koçboynuzu, or ram's horn motif, is a symbol of male fertility and power, woven by women to give strength and courage to their husbands. The yildiz, or eight-pointed star motif, generally expresses happiness, but is often expanded and adapted to create large motifs bearing little resemblance to a star. Nazarlik, göz, çengel and haç are all motifs that protect against the 'evil eye'. The people of central Asia believe that a look from the evil eye can injure, or even kill, and many of the kilim motifs protect against it.

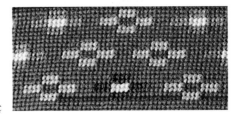

Haç

DESIGNS FROM
Afghanistan

....

Afghanistan is a country of dramatically contrasting
landscapes, whose deserts and mountains have
attracted travellers and conquerors from the earliest
times. Though Afghanistan is thought to be one
of the original centres of loom weaving, its wonderful
kilims were largely overlooked by the West until the
arrival of 'hippie' travellers in the early sixties.

The troubled history of Afghanistan has brought
together a great diversity of ethnic groups, and,
consequently, an equally varied range of kilim designs.
From the dark-banded kilims of the Baluchi, to the
vivacious, bright geometry of the Uzbek kilims,
and the rich, deep-red designs from Mukkur, the
people of Afghanistan produce an amazing variety
of stunning styles for us to stitch in needlepoint.

....

Mukkur Cushion

Mukkur (pronounced Mudjur), a market town in southern Afghanistan, is the traditional gathering place for a colourful group of wanderers known as Kutchi. The Kutchi are the gypsies of central Asia, who earn their living as tinkers and traders. The intricate kilim designs that reflect their love of ornament and embellishment are adorned with mirror sequins, brightly coloured beads, shells and ornate tassels.

Image size: 209 x 207 stitches, 44·2 x 43·8cm (17³/₈ x 17¹/₄in)

MATERIALS

56cm (22in) square of
   12-count canvas
Anchor tapestry wool:
   18 skeins of 8204
   15 skeins of 9800
   5 skeins of 8202
   4 skeins of 8000
   3 skeins of 9444, 9446
   1 skein of 8740, 9064, 9066
size 20 tapestry needle
scissors
48 x 61cm (19 x 24in) of
   black velvet
pins
tacking thread
sewing needle
matching sewing thread
45cm (18in) cushion pad
2m (2¹/₈yd) of black cord
4 tassels (optional – to make
your own, see pages 123–4)

TO STITCH

Before stitching, it is advisable to read the sections 'Materials and Equipment' and 'Techniques'. Begin stitching in one corner, 5cm (2in) from the edge. Work the needlepoint in tent stitch, using a single strand of tapestry wool, and following the chart overleaf. Stitch the first half of the design as given on the chart, then turn the chart 180 degrees to stitch the other half of the design, matching the centre lines (see page 116). Once the stitching is complete, stretch the needlepoint, as shown on pages 116–17.

TO MAKE UP

1 Make a 1·5cm (⁵/₈in) hem along both short edges of the velvet. Cut the velvet in half lengthways. With right sides facing, pin one cut edge to the left-hand side of the canvas and the other cut edge to the right-hand edge of the canvas. Overlap the two velvet panels and tack through all layers round the edge of the needlepoint.
2 Machine stitch round the edge of the needlepoint, leaving a small gap in the centre of the bottom edge for turning. Trim the canvas to 1cm (¹/₂in) and the velvet to 1·5cm (⁵/₈in). Trim across the corners to reduce bulk and turn the cover right sides out.
3 Tuck one end of the cord into the gap and stitch securely in place. Slipstitch the cord to the edge of the cushion, all round. Trim the cord, if necessary, tuck the end into the gap, and slipstitch the gap closed. If you would like to add tassels, stitch them firmly to the corners.

KEY

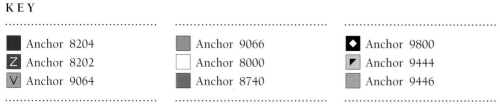

■ Anchor 8204	■ Anchor 9066	◆ Anchor 9800
Z Anchor 8202	☐ Anchor 8000	▸ Anchor 9444
V Anchor 9064	■ Anchor 8740	■ Anchor 9446

Khorasan Bags

Khorasan, which means 'Land of the Rising Sun', is a fertile valley with lush pastures on Afghanistan's border with Iran. The valley is on the ancient silk route, so Khorasan became home to many former nomadic peoples from western Afghanistan. The sombre, rich colours of their kilims are similar to kilims made by the Baluchi and Aimaq people. The exquisite designs for this pair of small bags were inspired by the ornate border of a beautiful nineteenth-century rug. The original has a variegated effect produced by variations in the dyes, and the bags echo this by mixing different coloured threads in the needle.

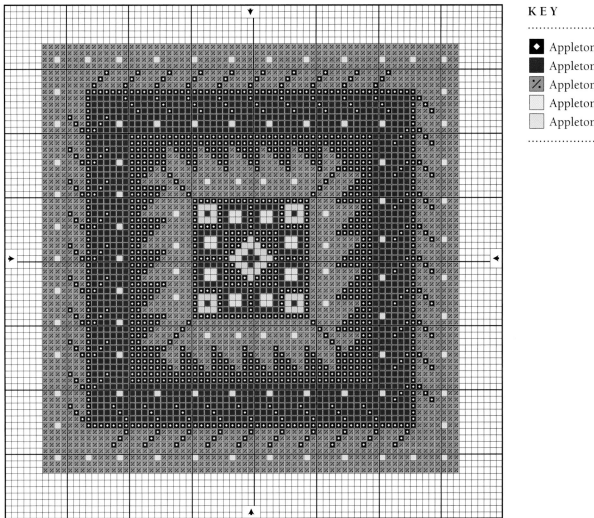

KEY

....

◆ Appleton 328 + 327

■ Appleton 209

⧄ Appleton 205 + 207

☐ Appleton 701

☐ Appleton 692

....

Image size: 67 x 67 stitches, 12·2 x 12·2cm (4³/₄ x 4³/₄in)

MATERIALS

....

For each bag

two 18cm (7in) squares of
   14-count canvas

Appleton crewel wool:
   2 skeins each of 205, 207,
     209, 327, 328, 692, 701

size 22 tapestry needle

scissors

18 x 36cm (7 x 14in) medium-
   weight cotton fabric

pins

matching sewing thread

sewing needle

....

TO STITCH

....

Before stitching, it is advisable to read the sections
'Materials and Equipment' and 'Techniques'. Begin
stitching in one corner, 2·5cm (1in) from the edge.
Work the needlepoint in tent stitch, using three
strands of crewel wool, and following the charts above
or overleaf. Where the chart indicates two colours
together, use two strands of one colour and one strand
of the second colour (reverse the colours every time
you start a new length, to produce a variegated effect).

    Stitch two panels from the chart, one each for front
and back of the bag. Once the stitching is complete,
stretch the needlepoint, as shown on pages 116–17.

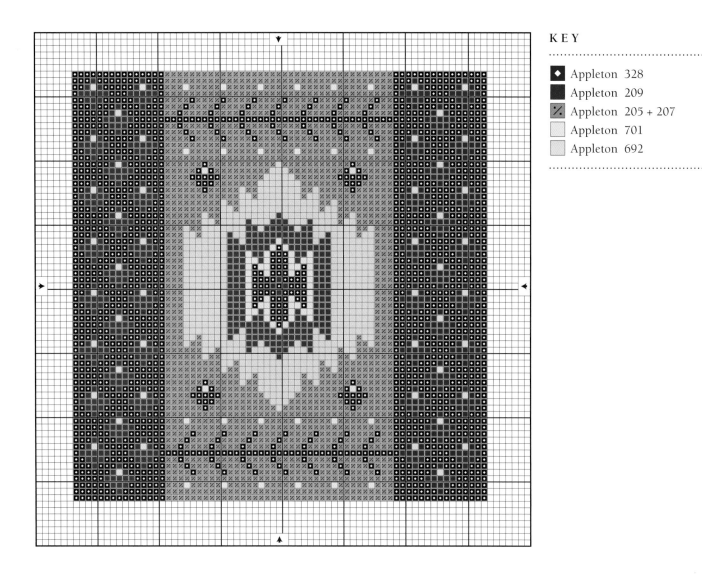

KEY
....

◆ Appleton 328

■ Appleton 209

% Appleton 205 + 207

☐ Appleton 701

☐ Appleton 692
....

TO MAKE UP
....

1 Cut the cotton fabric in two lengthways, to make two squares. Pin the squares of fabric to the canvas panels, right sides together. Machine stitch close to the edge of the needlepoint leaving a gap along the bottom edge for turning.

2 Trim the seam allowance to 1cm (¹/₂in), cut across the corners to reduce bulk and turn the panels right sides out. Slipstitch the gap and press on the reverse.

3 Pin the two panels together, with the needlepoint facing outwards. Oversew the sides and along the bottom edge with two strands of matching crewel wool.

4 Using several lengths of 205, 207 and 209, make a plaited cord (see page 123) long enough to form a strap that extends down the sides of the bag and hangs below the bottom edge to form tassels. Pin the plaited cord in position, and stitch it invisibly to the sides of the bag. Oversew the plaited cord to the top and bottom corners of the bag.

5 Wrap the plaited cord, level with the bottom of the bag, using matching yarn. Unravel the ends, then trim, to make tassels. Make two more small matching tassels (see pages 123–4) and stitch in place along the bottom edge.

Kazakh Purse

The Kazakh people were originally nomads and horse breeders. Wealthy Khans would have thousands of horses, and equally large numbers of tents and kilims. The ram's-horn motif popular with the Kazakhs is a symbol of masculinity and power, often used in designs for men, woven by their wives. Here, it has been used to make an unusual purse.

Image size: 140 x 76 stitches, 25·4 x 13·8cm (10 x 5³⁄₈in)

MATERIALS

30 x 20cm (12 x 8in) of 14-count canvas

Appleton crewel wool:
  3 skeins of 328, 358, 841
  2 skeins of 843, 865, 327, 331A
  1 skein of 866

size 22 tapestry needle
scissors
tacking thread
matching sewing thread
sewing needle
30 x 20cm (12 x 8in) of dark-blue cotton fabric

TO STITCH

Before stitching, it is advisable to read the sections 'Materials and Equipment' and 'Techniques'. Begin stitching in one corner, 2·5cm (1in) from the edge. Work the needlepoint in tent stitch, using three strands of crewel wool, and following the chart opposite.
If two colours are specified in the key, use two strands of one colour and one of the other. Once the stitching is complete, stretch the needlepoint, as shown on pages 116–17.

TO MAKE UP

1 Pin the cotton fabric to the canvas, right sides together. Stitch round the edge of the needlepoint, leaving a gap for turning.
2 Trim the canvas and fabric to 1cm (¹⁄₂in), and trim across the corners to reduce bulk. Turn right sides out. Slipstitch the gap closed. Press on the reverse side.
3 Fold the needlepoint in three, with the shaped end making the flap. With the flap open, tack the sides of the purse together. Oversew the edges of the purse using a double length of matching crewel wool.
4 To finish, make two tassels (see pages 123–4), and sew them securely to the inside top edges of the purse.

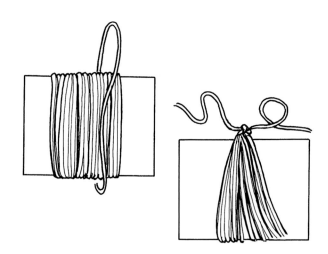

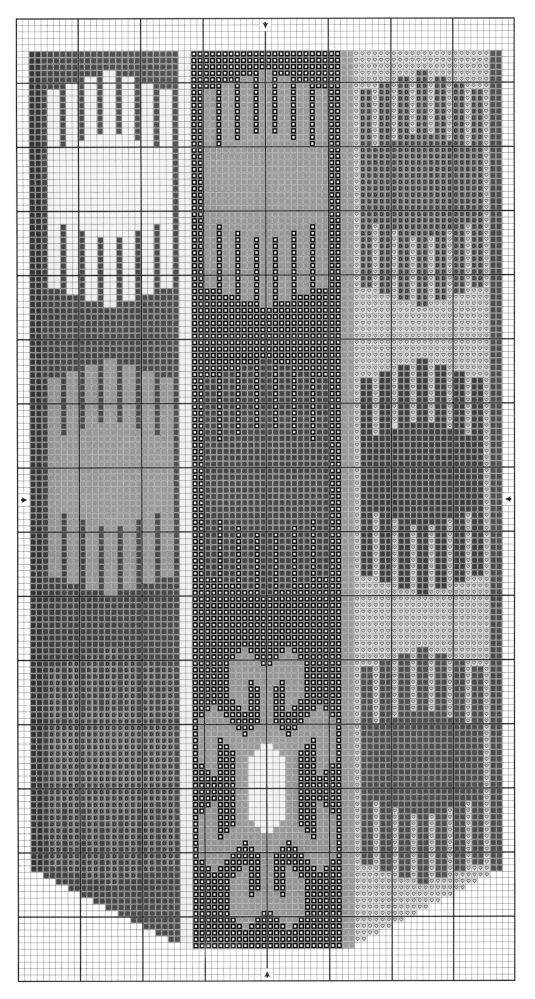

KEY

....

- ■ Appleton 328
- ◻ Appleton 327 + 328
- D Appleton 865
- ■ Appleton 866
- ■ Appleton 843
- ♡ Appleton 841 + 331A
- □ Appleton 841
- ■ Appleton 358

....

Namakdan Wallhanging

As the people of central Asia live far from the sea, rock salt is highly prized (for cooking and for their animals). The Baluchi and Uzbeks have many beliefs surrounding rock salt, and they weave unusual narrow-necked bags, called Namakdan, to transport and store the salt. The neck of the Namakdan bag folds down to prevent the salt from spilling and to protect the valuable contents. Traditionally, three special tassels are also attached to the bag, for luck. The Namakdan design has been adapted for a wallhanging, using the bag's unusual shape as a feature.

Image size: 146 x 168 stitches, 30·9 x 35·6cm (12³/₁₆ x 14in)

MATERIALS

....

40 x 46cm (16 x 18in) of
  12-count canvas
Anchor tapestry wool:
  6 skeins of 8330
  5 skeins of 8354, 8742
  4 skeins of 9502, 9768
size 20 tapestry needle
scissors

35 x 40cm (14 x 16in) of
  cotton fabric
pins
tacking thread
sewing needle
matching sewing thread
shells and beads (optional)

....

TO STITCH

....

Before stitching, it is advisable to read the sections 'Materials and Equipment' and 'Techniques'. Begin stitching in one corner, 5cm (2in) in from the edge. Work the needlepoint in tent stitch, using a single strand of tapestry wool, and following the chart overleaf. Once the stitching is complete, stretch the needlepoint, as shown on pages 116–17.

TO MAKE UP

....

1 Pin the backing fabric to the canvas, right sides together. Machine stitch round the edge of the needlepoint, leaving a gap at one end for turning. Trim the canvas and backing fabric to 1cm (½in). Trim across the corners to reduce bulk. Turn right sides out. Slipstitch the gap closed. Press the finished panel on the reverse side.

2 Make some decorative cords by plaiting leftover yarn (see page 123). Sew them to both sides of the 'neck' of the 'bag' to make a fringe, as shown. Wrap some of the cords with yarn in contrasting colours, and attach tassels, shells and beads (if using).

3 Make two more plaited cords, long enough to make loops, with extra hanging cord. Stitch the loops securely to the top corners of the wallhanging then unravel the ends to make tassels, or attach beads.

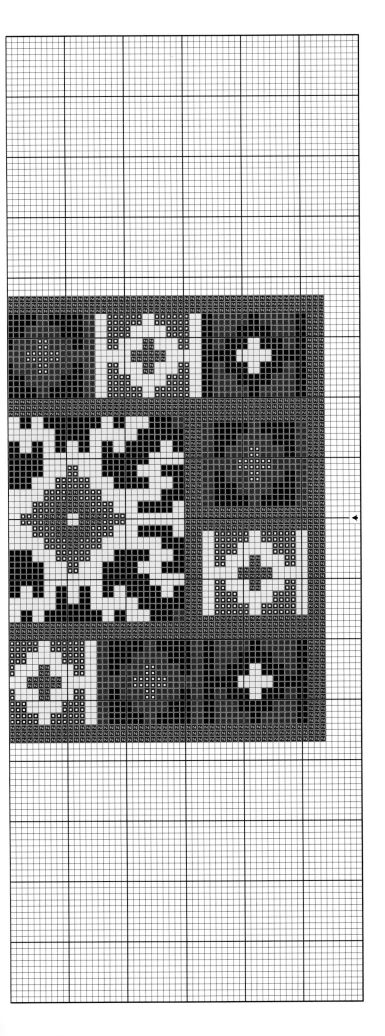

K E Y

▢	Anchor 9768
N	Anchor 8354
▓	Anchor 8330
■	Anchor 8742
░	Anchor 9502

Uzbek Book Cover

The Uzbeks cling to their traditional nomadic lifestyle with extraordinary determination, in spite of persistent persecution (they are a political rather than an ethnic group). They live in what is to us one of the remotest areas, and they weave brightly-coloured, vivacious, geometric designs to decorate their traditional round tent, the yurt. The diamond design chosen for this book cover is a typical example, with its apparently randomly-chosen colours. The design has been worked in coton perlé on finer canvas, to suit an A5 notebook, or Filofax. The repeating pattern can easily be extended to fit a larger book, in which case the quantities will need adapting.

Image size: 146 x 109 stitches, 26·5 x 19·8cm (10½ x 7¾in)

MATERIALS

....

28 x 20cm (11 x 8in) of
  14-count canvas
DMC coton perlé no. 3:
  4 skeins of 349
  2 skeins of 783, 930
  1 skein of blanc (white), 310,
    347, 355, 502, 640, 644,
    898, 945, 951
A5 notebook or Filofax

size 22 tapestry needle
scissors
20 x 61cm (8 x 24in) of
  black cotton poplin
pins
tacking thread
black sewing thread
sewing needle

....

TO STITCH

....

Open your book out flat, measure it, and adjust the
size of the canvas and chart accordingly. Before
stitching, it is advisable to read the sections 'Materials
and Equipment' and 'Techniques'. Work the design
in tent stitch, using a single strand of DMC coton perlé
no. 3, following the chart overleaf.

Check that the needlepoint fits over the cover of
the closed notebook. The tent stitch should come right
to the edge of the book. Stretch the needlepoint, as
shown on pages 116–17.

TO MAKE UP

....

1 Place the needlepoint centrally on the black fabric,
right sides facing. Machine stitch together down both
long sides. Trim the canvas to 1·5cm (⅝in) and turn
right sides out. Place on a flat surface, black fabric down.
2 To make each double-thickness flap, fold over a
small turning round the three edges of the black fabric,

then fold this flap of fabric in half to meet the edge of
the canvas. Pin and tack round the three sides of the
folded fabric. Stitch the black fabric to the edge of the
needlepoint using tiny hem stitches, and slipstitch the
other two sides. Repeat at the other end. (These flaps
are folded again to make the real flaps.)
3 To finish the flaps, fold the stitched fabric flaps to the
inside of the cover and pin in place. Hem the top and
bottom edges of each flap securely to the lining.

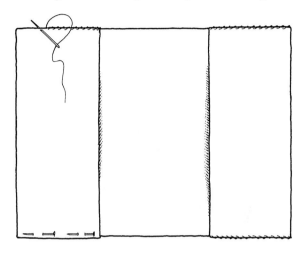

4 Make a decorative cord slightly longer than the
notebook by plaiting leftover yarn (see page 123). Make
a tassel at one end by unplaiting the ends and wrapping
with contrasting thread (see pages 123–4). Make three
tassels with contrasting wrapping and attach them
to the tasselled end of the cord, using contrasting
wrapping. Unpick a few stitches at the centre top of
the cover, tuck the untasselled end of the plait inside the
cover, and stitch securely. To finish, fit the cover of the
book inside the flaps.

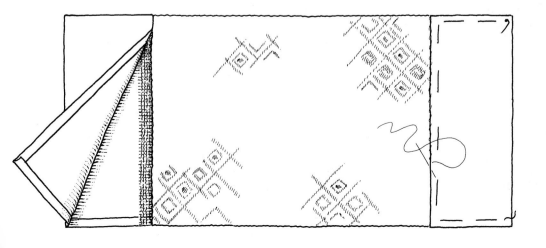

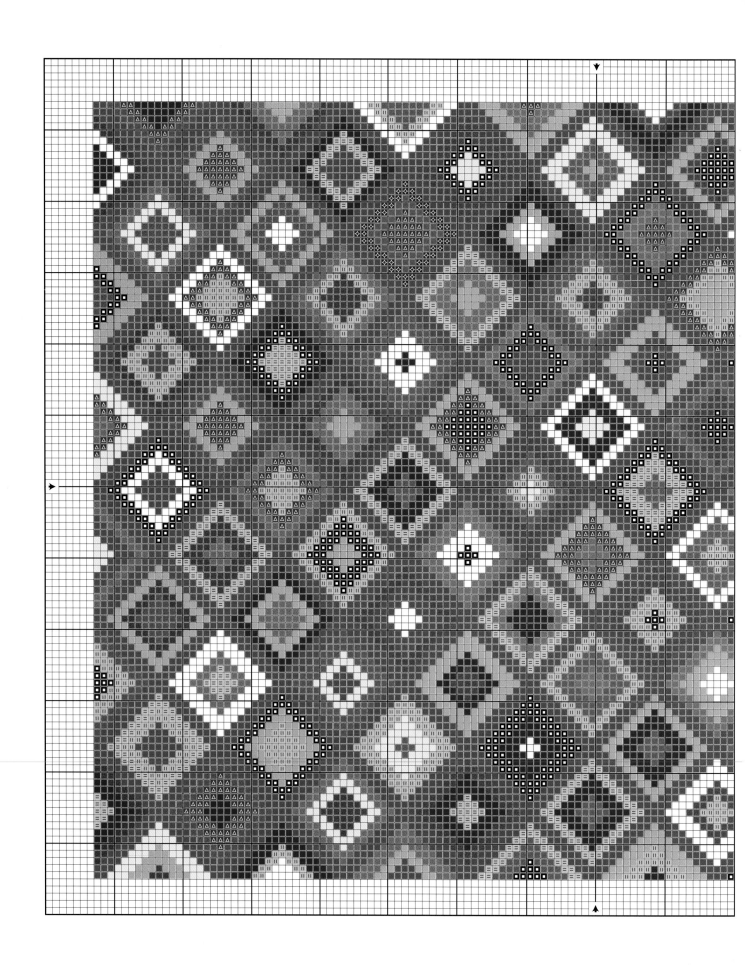

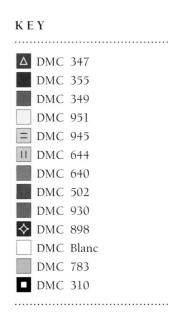

KEY
....

△ DMC 347
■ DMC 355
■ DMC 349
□ DMC 951
= DMC 945
II DMC 644
■ DMC 640
■ DMC 502
■ DMC 930
◇ DMC 898
□ DMC Blanc
■ DMC 783
□ DMC 310

....

Labijar Picnic Stool

Labijar is a fertile area of northern Afghanistan, which includes four villages. The Turkomen of Labijar would tell stories of successful hunting trips, and weave talismanic symbols into their kilims to illustrate their good fortune. The double-arrowhead design represents good luck in hunting, and the hour glass is a symbol of light and energy to help achieve success. The name 'Labijar' means 'next to the small river', so it seemed appropriate to use this design for a picnic or fishing stool. Note that you may need to adjust the design and the materials required to fit your chosen stool.

Image size (for stool shown): 228 x 141 stitches, 48·3 x 29·8cm (19 x 11¾in)

MATERIALS

61 x 43cm (24 x 17in) of
  12-count canvas
Anchor tapestry wool:
  8 skeins of 9306, 9402
  5 skeins of 8022, 8744
  4 skeins of 8354
  2 skeins of 8024, 8742, 9308
  1 skein of 8040, 8240, 8242,
   8740, 9216

size 20 tapestry needle
scissors
51 x 33cm (20 x 13in) of
  heavyweight, cotton fabric
pins
matching sewing thread
matching strong thread
sewing needle
picnic stool, of style shown

TO STITCH

If your chosen stool does not have the same image size as the one shown, measure the seat cover of your stool and adjust the chart to fit. Add 13cm (5in) to each dimension of the new image size to obtain the canvas size. The last few centimetres (inches) of canvas at each side wrap round the bars of the stool, so they can be a fairly plain part of the design.

Before stitching, it is advisable to read the sections 'Materials and Equipment' and 'Techniques'. Begin stitching in one corner of the canvas, 7cm (2½in) from the edge. Work the needlepoint in tent stitch, using a single strand of tapestry wool, and following the chart overleaf. Once the stitching is complete, stretch the needlepoint, as shown on pages 116–17.

TO MAKE UP

1 Pin the cotton fabric to the canvas, right sides together. Machine stitch round the edge of the needlepoint, leaving a gap at one end for turning. Stitch along the long edges a second time, for extra strength. Trim the canvas and fabric to 1cm (½in), and trim across the corners to reduce bulk. Turn right sides out. Slipstitch the gap closed. Press the finished seat panel on the reverse side.

2 Wrap one short edge of the panel round one short side of the stool, and pin in place. Stitch the edge of the panel to the underside of the seat using hemming stitches. Stitch into the needlepoint, but be careful not to let the stitches show on the right side. Hem again in the opposite direction to make small cross stitches. Stitch the thread ends in securely. Repeat step 2 to attach the other end of the seat panel.

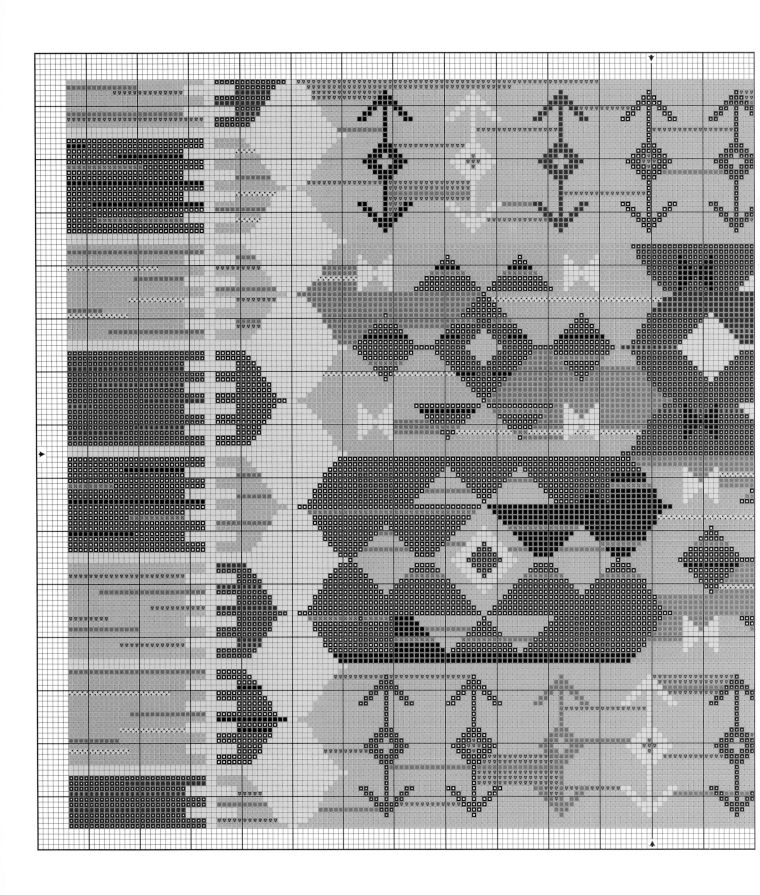

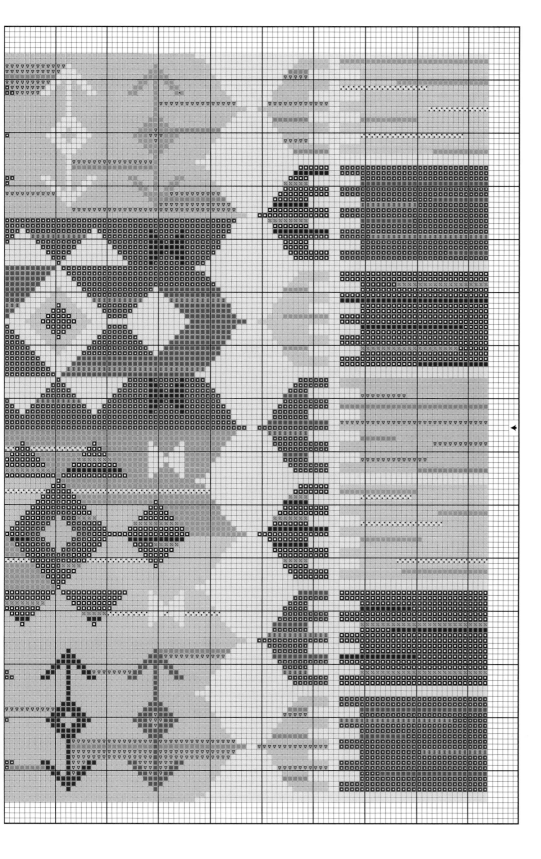

K E Y
....

⬤ Anchor 8354

▪ Anchor 8242

Ⅱ Anchor 8240

▫ Anchor 8744

■ Anchor 8742

⁄∕ Anchor 8740

▪ Anchor 8024

▫ Anchor 8022

•⦁ Anchor 8040

▪ Anchor 9216

▽ Anchor 9308

▫ Anchor 9306

▫ Anchor 9402
....

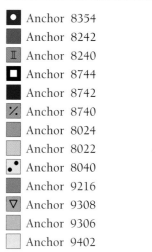

Farah Wallhanging

In the town of Farah, on the river Farah, the Taimani Aimaq people live in encampments of unusual square or rectangular yurts. The colours and motifs used in the Taimani Aimaq kilims are influenced by those of the neighbouring Baluchi. This design comes originally from a tent band, and has the typical eight-pointed star of Anatolian kilims, symbolizing happiness. Here, the original muted complementary colours are highlighted by the use of white, and the chart has been repeated to make a narrow hanging.

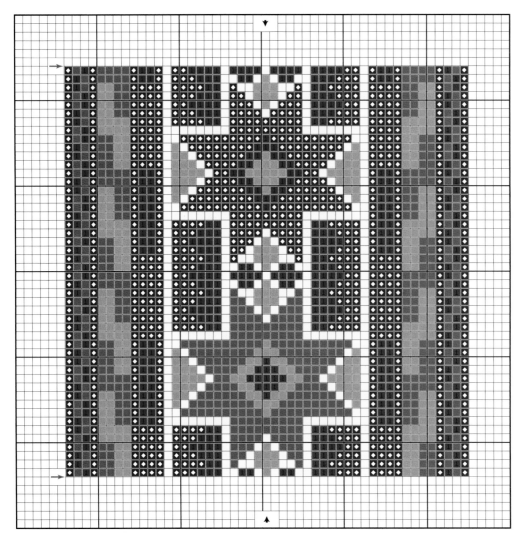

Image size: 216 x 49 stitches, 45·8 x 10·4cm (18 x 4in)

MATERIALS

51 x 15cm (20 x 6in) of
  12-count canvas
Anchor tapestry wool:
  4 skeins of 9684
  3 skeins of 9680
  2 skeins of 8032, 8442, 9064
size 20 tapestry needle
scissors
51 x 15cm (20 x 6in) of
  cotton fabric
pins
matching sewing thread
sewing needle
bell-pull end (dowel type)
craft knife
paint in chosen colour for
  bell-pull end (optional)

KEY

◆ Anchor 9684   ▨ Anchor 9064

1 Anchor 8442   ■ Anchor 9680

☐ Anchor 8032   → repeat

TO STITCH

Before stitching, it is advisable to read the sections 'Materials and Equipment' and 'Techniques'. Begin stitching in one corner, 2·5cm (1in) from the edge. Work the needlepoint in tent stitch, using a single strand of tapestry wool, and following the chart opposite. Repeat the design four-and-a-half times to make the wallhanging as shown. Once the stitching is complete, stretch the needlepoint, as shown on pages 116–17.

TO MAKE UP

1 Pin the cotton fabric to the canvas, right sides facing. Machine stitch together down one side, along the bottom and up the other side, close to the edge of the needlepoint, starting and finishing 2·5cm (1in) from the top edge.

2 Trim the seam allowance to 1cm (¹/₂in) and cut across the bottom corners to reduce bulk before turning right sides out. Press the needlepoint on the reverse side.

3 Turn under the top edges of the canvas and lining and slipstitch securely together along the top edge, leaving the sides open to form a channel for the bell-pull end.

4 Remove one knob from the bell-pull end, and trim the dowel to fit the needlepoint, using a craft knife. Paint the bell-pull end, if required. Once the paint is dry, slide the dowel through the channel in the hanging and place the knob on the bell-pull end.

5 Make a 40cm (16in) cord from dark-brown yarn (see page 123). Open out the cord, and slip over the dowel, tying a knot underneath to secure. Make two 20cm (8in) lengths of green cord and tie round the dowel, to hang at different lengths. Add tassels to the ends of the cords (see pages 123–4). Trim the tassels, unravel the wool to make finer strands, dampen these strands, twist them to remove excess water, and leave to dry.

Malaki Rug

The Baluchi Malaki are nomads who live in an area near the Dasht-i-Margo, the 'Desert of Death'. Their kilims are usually very dark and rich in appearance, and, because this depth of colour is time-consuming to produce, the kilims in the darkest colours are the most valuable. The complicated pattern that created the inspiration for this project is typical of the rugs woven by young girls for their dowries. It has been stitched in tent stitch, but you could use cross stitch, if preferred. Note that, because of its size, this rug is best stitched on a frame.

Image size: 183 x 277 stitches, 66·4 x 100·7cm (26 x 39¾in)

MATERIALS

80 x 115cm (31 x 45in) of
   7-count interlock canvas
Anchor tapestry wool:
   24 skeins of 9682, 9684
   12 skeins of 8744, 8220
   8 skeins of 8032, 9680
   2 skeins of 9362

size 18 tapestry needle
scissors
75 x 115cm (30 x 45in) of
   heavyweight cotton fabric
pins
matching strong thread
sewing needle

TO STITCH

Fit the canvas onto your frame. If your frame is not wide enough, make the rug in two sections joined down the centre (see page 117). Alternatively, if your frame has dowels attached by dowel screws and wing nuts, you could replace the existing dowels with two longer lengths of dowel.

   Before stitching, it is advisable to read the sections 'Materials and Equipment' and 'Techniques'. Begin stitching at one of the top corners, 7cm (3in) from the edge. Work the design in tent stitch, using two strands of tapestry wool, and following the chart overleaf. (If you prefer to work this design in cross stitch, use a single strand of tapestry wool, and make sure that the top stitches all face in the same direction.)

   Stitch the first half of the design as given on the chart, then turn the chart 180 degrees to stitch the other half of the design, matching the centre lines (see page 116).

Once complete, stretch the needlepoint, as shown on pages 116–17. As the rug is quite large, you may need to stretch it on the floor in the corner of a spare room. Lay the needlepoint on a white sheet, and use strong pins stuck through the canvas and into the carpet/floor at an angle.

TO MAKE UP

1 Trim the excess canvas to 2·5cm (1in). Cut the heavyweight cotton fabric to the same size as the trimmed canvas. Turn the excess canvas to the reverse side, mitre the corners and tack in place.
2 Cut 30cm (12in) lengths of wool and attach to one end of the rug to make a fringe, as shown on pages 121–2. (You could attach a fringe to both ends, if preferred.)
3 Press the seam allowance of the backing fabric to the wrong side, mitre the corners and tack. Pin the backing fabric to the reverse side of the rug. Slipstitch the edges of the fabric and the canvas together.
4 Work rows of running stitches about 30cm (12in) apart across the back of the rug into the canvas, to attach the backing fabric to the needlepoint. Take care not to let the stitches show on the right side. If you prefer a knotted or net fringe use longer lengths of wool and trim neatly once complete.
5 Hang the rug using one of the methods described on pages 120–1.

● Anchor 9682
⊠ Anchor 9680
☐ Anchor 9684
■ Anchor 8744
■ Anchor 8220
▽ Anchor 8032
☐ Anchor 9362

Ersari Cushion

The Ersari Turkomen were originally nomadic, but now they live in tents only during the summer, when they move to summer grazing with their flocks. In the winter, they live in villages. Their exquisitely ornate kilims and bags are an essential part of this semi-nomadic lifestyle, and the different peoples use distinctive güls (flower-like medallions) to reflect their individual identities.

Image size: 211 x 207 stitches, 44·7 x 43·8cm (17⅝ x 17¼in)

MATERIALS

....

56cm (22in) square of
  12-count canvas
Anchor Tapestry wool:
  17 skeins of 8218
  15 skeins of 9800
  5 skeins of 8216
  3 skeins of 9442, 9444, 9446
  2 skeins of 8006
  1 skein of 8604, 9064, 9066
size 20 tapestry needle
scissors
48 x 61cm (19 x 24in) of
  black velvet
pins
tacking thread
sewing needle
black sewing thread
45cm (18in) cushion pad
2m (2⅛yd) of black cord
4 tassels (optional – to make
your own, see pages 123–4)

....

TO STITCH

....

Before stitching, it is advisable to read the sections 'Materials and Equipment' and 'Techniques'. Begin stitching in one corner, 5cm (2in) from the edge. Work the needlepoint in tent stitch, using a single strand of tapestry wool, and following the chart on pages 44–7. Once the stitching is complete, stretch the needlepoint, as shown on pages 116–17.

TO MAKE UP

....

1 Make a 1·5cm (⅝in) hem along both short edges of the velvet. Cut the velvet in half lengthways. With right sides facing, pin one cut edge to the left-hand side of the canvas and the other cut edge to the right-hand edge of the canvas. Overlap the two velvet panels and tack through all layers round the edge of the needlepoint.
2 Machine stitch round the edge of the needlepoint, leaving a small gap in the centre of the bottom edge for turning. Trim the canvas to 1cm (½in) and the velvet to 1·5cm (⅝in). Trim across the corners to reduce bulk and turn the cover right sides out.
3 Tuck one end of the cord into the gap and stitch securely in place. Slipstitch the cord to the edge of the cushion, all round. Trim the cord, if necessary, tuck the end into the gap, and slipstitch the gap closed. If you would like to add tassels, stitch them firmly to the corners.

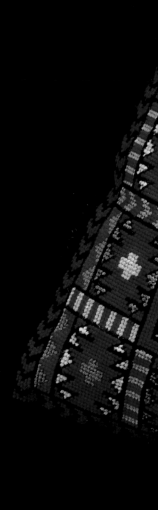

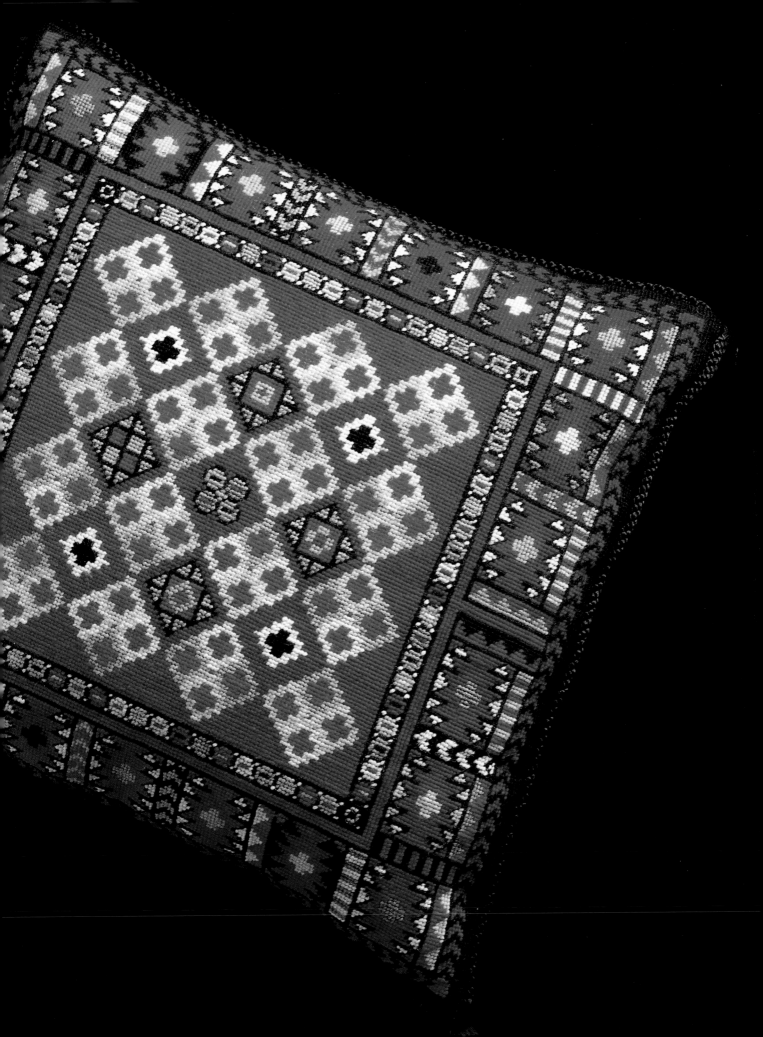

KEY

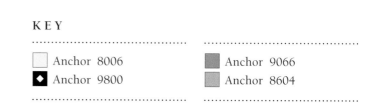

☐ Anchor 8006
◆ Anchor 9800

■ Anchor 9066
■ Anchor 8604

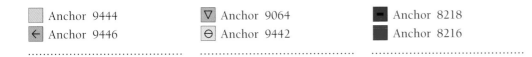

Anchor 9444

← Anchor 9446

▽ Anchor 9064

⊖ Anchor 9442

▬ Anchor 8218

▮ Anchor 8216

DESIGNS FROM
Anatolia

·····················

Anatolia is the Asian part of Turkey, bordered
on one side by the Black Sea, and on the other side
by the Mediterranean, thus forming a 'bridge'
between the continents of Europe and Asia.
The resulting mixture of cultures and religions has
produced a kilim tradition rich in colour, pattern
and motif; from the sacred ram's-horn kilims of
Yüncü, to the delightful cypress-tree designs
from Keçimuhsine, and the unusual multiple
prayer-niche rugs from Karapinar.

·····················

Konya Rug

The splendid kilims of Konya are easily recognized by their cheerful colouring and bold geometric patterns. The delightful double bird-wing motif, often used in a border, is one of the most distinctive kilim patterns. The bird is believed to be the bearer of good tidings, happiness, joy and love. The yildiz, or star motif, which also expresses happiness, has been expanded to create a magnificent central motif for the rug design. Note that, because of its size, this project is best stitched on a frame.

Image size: 162 x 198 stitches, 41·2 x 50·3cm (16$^1/_5$ x 19$^4/_5$in)

MATERIALS

50 x 60 cm (20 x 24in) of
  10-count canvas
Anchor tapestry wool:
  10 skeins of 8032
  6 skeins of 9602
  5 skeins of 8742, 9362
  4 skeins of 9600
  3 skeins of 8740, 9330
  2 skeins of 8060, 8738, 9326,
    9364, 9598
  1 skein of 9328
size 20 tapestry needle
scissors
50 x 60cm (20 x 24in)
  heavyweight cotton fabric
pins
tacking thread
matching sewing thread
sewing needle

TO STITCH

Before stitching, it is advisable to read the sections 'Materials and Equipment' and 'Techniques'. Begin at the top of the canvas 4cm (1$^1/_2$in) from the edge. Work the needlepoint in tent stitch, using a single strand of tapestry wool, and following the chart overleaf. (Depending on the width of your frame, the design can be stitched vertically or horizontally.)

Stitch the first half of the design as given on the chart, then turn the chart 180 degrees to stitch the other half of the design, matching the centre lines (see page 116). Once the stitching is complete, stretch the needlepoint, as shown on pages 116–17.

TO MAKE UP

1 Trim the excess canvas to 2·5cm (1in). Cut the cotton fabric to the same size as the trimmed canvas. Trim across the corners of the canvas to reduce bulk, turn the excess canvas to the reverse side and tack in place.
2 Cut 30cm (12in) lengths of 8032 and 9362 and attach them to both ends of the rug to make a fringe, as shown on pages 121–2.
3 Press the seam allowance of the cotton fabric to the wrong side. Mitre the corners and tack all round. Pin the fabric to the reverse side of the rug. Slipstitch the edges of the fabric and the canvas together.
4 Work rows of running stitches about 20cm (8in) apart across the back of the rug into the canvas, to attach the backing fabric to the needlepoint. Take care not to let the stitches show on the right side.

KEY

- ■ Anchor 8742
- ▣ Anchor 8740
- ■ Anchor 8738
- ← Anchor 9598
- ▽ Anchor 9600

- ■ Anchor 9602
- ◇ Anchor 8060
- ◤ Anchor 8032
- ▦ Anchor 9364

- □ Anchor 9362
- → Anchor 9326
- ↑ Anchor 9328
- ■ Anchor 9330

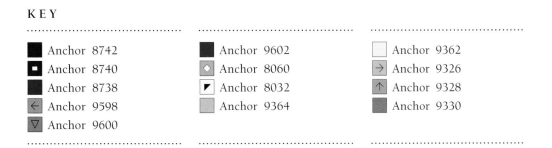

Manastir Chair Cushion

Kilims from Manastir are distinctive because they use a bright palette and small motifs. (To satisfy western tastes, kilims with such bright colours are usually faded in the sun for several months.) The design for the chair cushion has been adapted from a stylized star pattern on the border of a prayer kilim. The materials given below would make a seat pad approximately 36cm (14in) square.

Image size: 96 x 88 stitches, 20·3 x 18·6cm (8 x 7⁵⁄₁₆in)

MATERIALS

45cm (18in) square of
  12-count canvas
Anchor tapestry wool:
  12 skeins of 9768;
  5 skeins of 8204, 8058,
  9534, 9634;
  2 skeins of 9502, 9524,
  9766;
  1 skein of 8202, 8052

size 20 tapestry needle
scissors
45cm (18in) square of
  medium-weight cotton fabric
three pieces of 100g (4oz)
  wadding, each 40cm (16in)
pins
matching sewing thread
3m (3¼yd) of matching cord

TO STITCH

Before stitching, it is advisable to read the sections 'Materials and Equipment' and 'Techniques'. If your chair seat is not 36cm (14in), measure it and work out the size of your finished chair cushion. Plan the number of repeats required, allowing 4·5cm (1¾in) for each horizontal row of the design, and 5cm (2in) for the vertical columns. To ensure that the design is centred, start stitching in the centre, as follows. If there is an even number of motifs across the design, begin between two motifs. If there is an odd number, begin in the centre of a motif.

    Work the needlepoint in tent stitch, using a single strand of tapestry wool, and following the chart overleaf. Repeat the design as required to fill (see page 116). Once the stitching is complete, stretch the needlepoint, as shown on pages 116–17.

TO MAKE UP

1 Pin the cotton fabric to the canvas, right sides together. Machine stitch together round the edge of the needlepoint, leaving a gap along the back edge for turning. Trim the seam allowance to 1cm (½in) and cut across the corners to reduce bulk.

2 Turn the cushion cover right sides out. Trim the wadding pieces to the exact size of the cover and insert through the gap, tucking them right into the corners. Slipstitch the gap closed. Stitch several rows of running stitch across the back of the cushion to hold the wadding in place, making sure that the stitches do not show on the right side.

3 Cut a piece of cord to fit round the sides and front edge of the cushion, plus 50cm (20in) for tying, approximately 1·85m (2yd) in total. Position the cord and pin in place, beginning at the centre-front edge. Slipstitch the cord securely to the top edge of the cushion. Loop the cord at each corner and continue down the sides.

4 Cut a piece of cord to fit along the back edge, plus sufficient at each end for tying. Slipstitch the cord securely to the back edge of the cushion. Wrap the cords close to the corners for extra strength. Tie the cord in knots 5cm (2in) from the ends, and unravel them to make simple tassels. Alternatively, make a more ornate tassel to cover the knots (see pages 123–4).

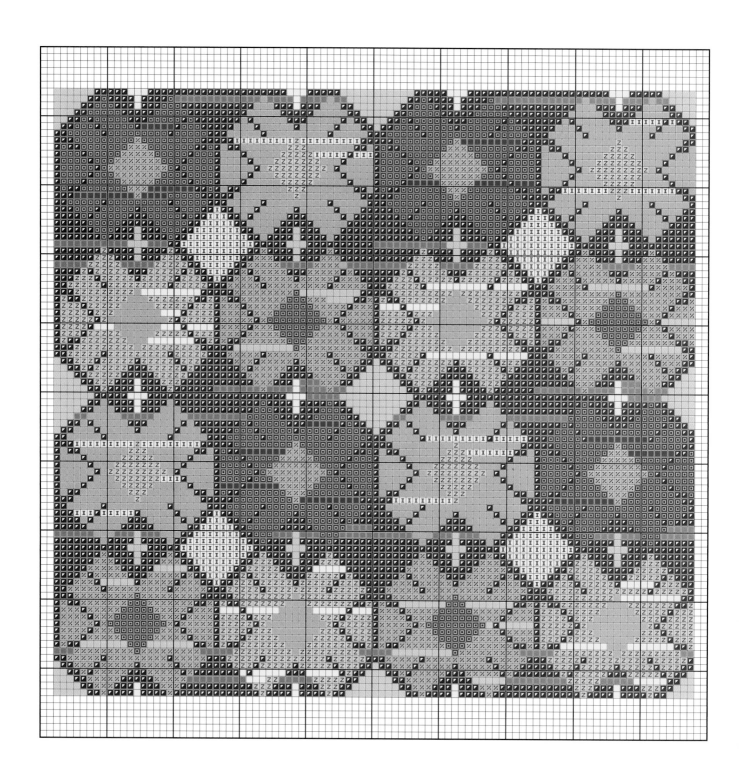

KEY

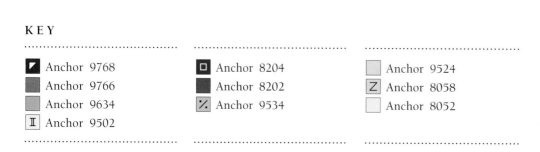

◤	Anchor 9768	☐	Anchor 8204		Anchor 9524
	Anchor 9766	◼	Anchor 8202	Z	Anchor 8058
	Anchor 9634	⁒	Anchor 9534		Anchor 8052
Ⅱ	Anchor 9502				

Karapinar Bolster Cushion

Karapinar is famous for its unusual prayer kilims, which have multiple prayer niches (not unlike Florentine work) down each side. Normally, a prayer kilim has one prayer niche, a triangular-shaped area known as the mihrab, that is pointed towards Mecca when praying. The design of the Karapinar prayer niches lends itself ideally to this bolster cushion.

Image size: 280 x 94 stitches, 59·2 x 19·9cm (23³/₈ x 7⁷/₈in)

MATERIALS

. . . .

70 x 30cm (27 x 12in) of
   12-count canvas
Anchor tapestry wool:
   9 skeins of 8034
   5 skeins of 8264, 9682
   2 skeins of 8054, 8258,
     8262, 8610, 9674, 9676
   1 skein of 9680
size 20 tapestry needle
scissors

70 x 115cm (28 x 45in) of
   medium-weight cotton fabric
45cm (18in) bolster-cushion
   pad, 17cm (6³/₄in) diameter
pins
tacking thread
needle
matching sewing thread
1·25m (1¹/₃yd) of piping cord
strong thread
2 large tassels

TO STITCH

. . . .

Before stitching, it is advisable to read the sections
'Materials and Equipment' and 'Techniques'.
The design is made up by working two repeats of the
chart side by side to make a narrow panel 60cm (24in)
long. Begin stitching 5cm (2in) from the edge. Work
the needlepoint in tent stitch, using a single strand of
tapestry wool, and following the chart opposite.
Once the stitching is complete, stretch the needlepoint,
as shown on pages 116–17.

TO MAKE UP

. . . .

1 Trim the excess canvas to 1·5cm (⁵/₈in). For the
side panels, cut two pieces of cotton fabric 18 x 63cm
(7 x 25in). For the gathered end panels of the cushion,
cut two pieces of fabric 12 x 63cm (5 x 25in).
2 Pin the fabric pieces for the side panels to the sides
of the canvas, right sides together and machine stitch
close to the needlepoint.
3 Cut two 5cm (2in) bias strips from the cotton fabric,
each 70cm (28in) long. Fold the bias strips over 70cm
(28in) lengths of piping cord, and tack to hold in place.
Pin the piping along both ends of the cushion cover
(see page 119).
4 Sew two rows of gathering stitches down one long
side of each end panel. Attach the other long edge to
the cushion cover, on top of the piping. Machine stitch
close to the piping cord using a zipper foot.

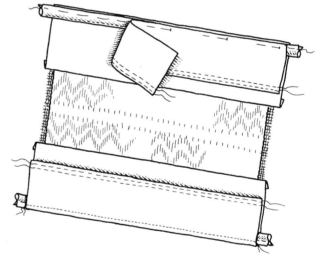

5 Fold the cushion cover in half lengthways, right
sides together. Match the seams, and pin. (Pin the bias
strip to different sides to avoid stitching through
too many layers.) Leaving the centre canvas panel
unstitched to make a gap for turning, stitch the seams
on both sides.
6 Gather up the end panels as tightly as possible.
Insert one tassel loop through each hole from the inside,
then wrap the gathers very tightly around the loops
using strong thread.
7 Turn the cushion cover right sides out. Insert the
cushion pad through the gap. Oversew the seam.

KEY

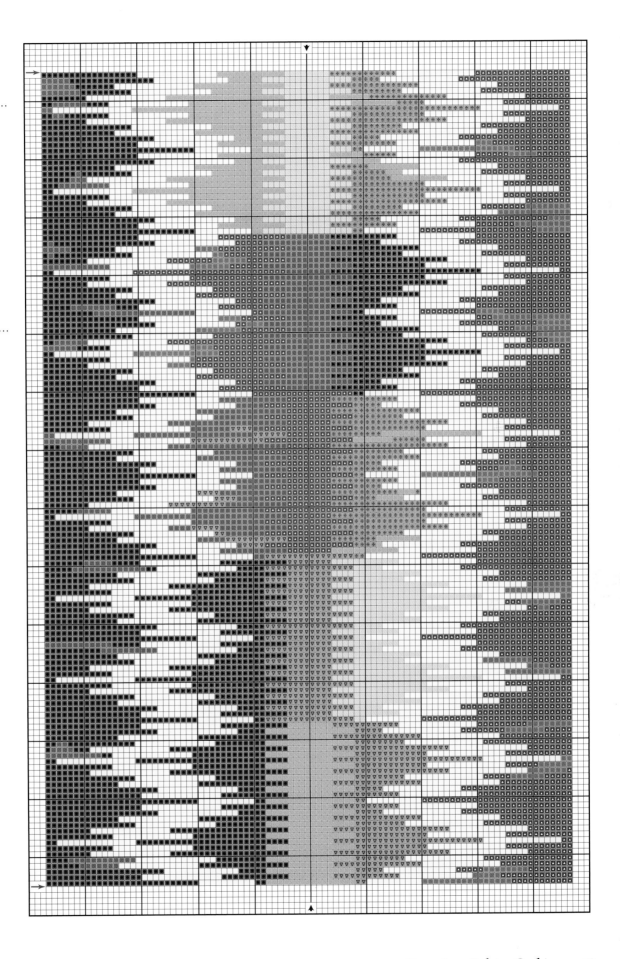

	Anchor 9674
÷	Anchor 9676
	Anchor 9680
▲	Anchor 9682
▽	Anchor 8258
	Anchor 8262
✦	Anchor 8264
	Anchor 8054
	Anchor 8034
▶	Anchor 8610
→	repeat

Yüncü Wallhanging

The style of traditional Yüncü kilims is unique. In the centre, they have a distinctive tree or pole, with extending arms. At the ends of these arms there are ram's-horn motifs (koçboynuzu). Sheep were of central importance to the once-nomadic Yüncü Yörük people, so the ram's-horn motif became a symbol of power, heroism and eternity. Here, the motif and the Yüncü design has inspired an impressive wallhanging.

Image size: 173 x 185 stitches, 36·6 x 39·4cm (14^1/$_2$ x 15^1/$_2$in)

MATERIALS

....

46 x 50cm (18 x 20in) of
  12-count canvas
Anchor tapestry wool:
  14 skeins of 8264
  9 skeins of 8840
  5 skeins of 8878
  2 skeins of 8260, 8262
  1 skein of 8880, 8882, 8884,
    8836, 8900, 8292, 9402,
    9404, 9406

size 20 tapestry needle
40 x 46cm (16 x 18in) of
  medium-weight cotton fabric
scissors
pins
matching sewing thread
sewing needle
approx. 15 each of blue and
  rust terracotta beads

....

TO STITCH

....

Before stitching, it is advisable to read the sections 'Materials and Equipment' and 'Techniques'. Begin stitching at the top of the canvas, 4cm (1^1/$_2$in) from the edge. Work the needlepoint in tent stitch, using a single strand of tapestry wool, and following the chart overleaf.

    Stitch the first half of the design as given on the chart, then turn the chart 180 degrees to stitch the other half of the design, matching the centre lines (see page 116). Once the stitching is complete, stretch the needlepoint, as shown on pages 116–17.

TO MAKE UP

....

1 Trim the excess canvas to 2·5cm (1in). Cut the cotton fabric to the same size as the trimmed canvas. Pin the fabric and needlepoint together, right sides facing. Machine stitch together, close to the edge of the needlepoint, leaving a gap along the bottom edge for turning.

2 Trim the seam allowance to 1cm (^{1}/$_2$in) and cut across the corners to reduce bulk. Turn right sides out, and slipstitch the gap closed. Press on the reverse side of the needlepoint.

3 Work rows of running stitch about 20cm (8in) apart across the back of the wallhanging, to hold the backing fabric on to the needlepoint. Make sure that the stitches do not show on the right side.

4 Cut 30cm (12in) lengths of wool and attach them to the bottom edge of the wallhanging to make a fringe, as shown on pages 121–2. Make several bundles of six strands of wool each, and plait them together. Thread the beads on the ends of these plaited cords, alternating rust and blue beads, and trim neatly.

5 Attach the wallhanging to the wall with a hidden fastening, or hang it from a dowel (see page 121).

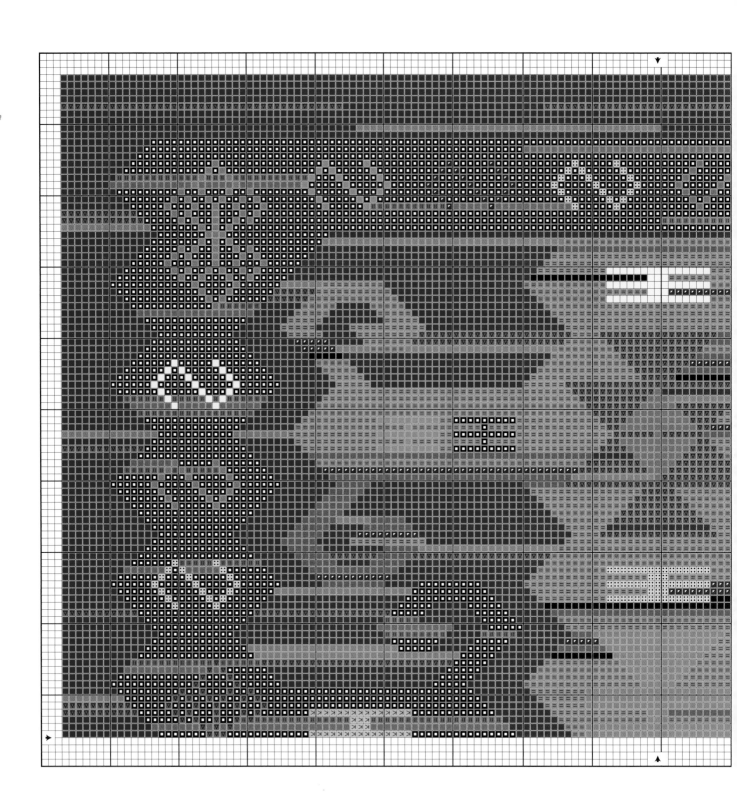

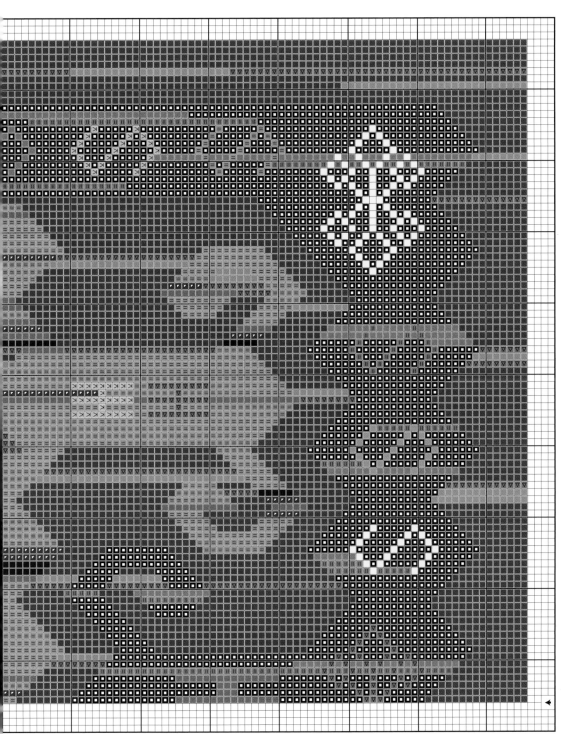

KEY

....

=	Anchor 8878
▓	Anchor 8880
◤	Anchor 8882
■	Anchor 8884
▦	Anchor 8836
‖	Anchor 8900
◻	Anchor 8840
▦	Anchor 8260
▽	Anchor 8262
▓	Anchor 8264
☐	Anchor 8292
⋰	Anchor 9402
⋊	Anchor 9404
▨	Anchor 9406

....

Keçimuhsine Spectacles Case

The kilims from Keçimuhsine, in central Anatolia, have a generally light appearance, often with a distinctive cypress-tree motif, on a white ground. The cypress tree is a symbol of eternity, sometimes known as the 'tree of life'. (It is often hung upside-down, so that the roots are closer to heaven.) The small, highly-prized, Keçimuhsine kilims, called çiçims from a Turkish word meaning 'small and delightful', provided the inspiration for this attractive spectacles case.

Image size: 45 x 92 stitches, 8·2cm x 16·7cm (3¹/₄ x 6⁵/₈in)

MATERIALS

....

26 x 30cm (10 x 12in) of
  12-count canvas
Appleton crewel wool:
  8 skeins of 992
  2 skeins of 325
  1 skein of 503, 998
size 20 tapestry needle
scissors
26cm (10in) square of cream,
  medium-weight, cotton
  fabric
26cm (10in) square of
  medium-weight, iron-on
  interfacing
tacking thread
pins
tailor's chalk
matching sewing thread
sewing needle

....

TO STITCH

Before stitching, it is advisable to read the sections 'Materials and Equipment' and 'Techniques'. Cut the canvas in half lengthways to make front and back pieces, each 26 x 15cm (10 x 6in). On each piece, begin stitching in one corner, 3cm (1¼in) from the edge. Work the needlepoint using four strands of crewel wool, following the chart (right). (Alternatively, you could use a single strand of tapestry wool). Once the stitching is complete, stretch the needlepoint, as shown on pages 116–17.

TO MAKE UP

1 Trim the excess canvas round the needlepoint to 1cm (½in). Snip into the corners, turn the excess canvas to the reverse side and tack in place.

2 Transfer the outline of the spectacle case to the interfacing using tailor's chalk. Cut two identical pieces, cutting just inside the outline. Place these on the reverse side of the cream fabric, with a 1cm (½in) seam allowance round each one. Iron to fix the interfacing to the fabric. Cut out, remembering the seam allowance. Snip into the corners, turn the seam allowance under and tack in place.

3 With reverse sides facing, pin the interfaced fabric pieces on the needlepoint front and back pieces. Slipstitch together round the edges. Pin the lined front and back together. Oversew together along the sides and bottom, using two strands of white crewel wool, starting and finishing 5cm (2in) from the top edge.

4 Make six simple tassels using twelve 10cm (4in) lengths of red, grey and blue wool (see pages 123–4). Tie the tassels using a double length of contrasting wool, which is then knotted to make a 1cm (½in) section of cord above the tassel. Sew three tassels onto each side of the spectacles case, at 3cm (1¼in) intervals, as shown.

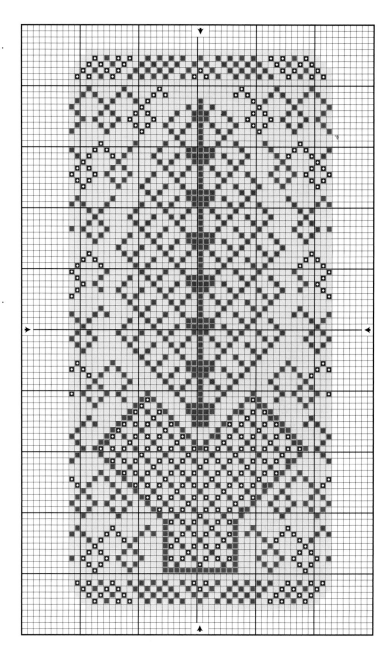

KEY

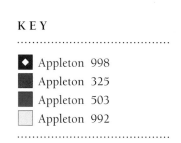

◆ Appleton 998
■ Appleton 325
■ Appleton 503
☐ Appleton 992

Parmakli Cushion

Parmakli are finger-shaped designs popular in the Afyon region of Anatolia, where they are believed to guard against evil. The parmakli appear in different forms decorating güls (medallions) and prayer niches, or protruding from square and rectangular shapes, which makes them ideal for this rectangular cushion.

Image size: 179 x 134 stitches, 37·9 x 28·4cm (15 x 11¹/₄in)

MATERIALS

....

50 x 40cm (20 x 16in) of
   12-count canvas
Anchor tapestry wool:
   4 skeins of 8032, 8242
   3 skeins of 8240, 8836, 8840
   2 skeins of 8238, 8902,
     8904, 9508, 9512
   1 skein of 8838, 8900, 9510
size 20 tapestry needle
scissors
56 x 40cm (22 x 16in) of
   medium-weight cotton fabric
pins
matching sewing thread
sewing needle
40 x 30cm (16 x 12in)
   cushion pad

....

TO STITCH

....

Before stitching, it is advisable to read the sections 'Materials and Equipment' and 'Techniques'. Begin stitching in one corner, 5cm (2in) from the edge. Work the needlepoint in tent stitch, using a single strand of tapestry wool, and following the chart overleaf. Once the stitching is complete, stretch the needlepoint, as shown on pages 116–17.

TO MAKE UP

....

1 Make a 1·5cm (⁵/₈in) hem along both short edges of the cotton fabric. Cut the fabric in half lengthways. With right sides facing, pin one cut edge to the left-hand side of the canvas and the other cut edge to the right-hand edge of the canvas. Overlap the two fabric panels and tack through all layers round the edge of the needlepoint.
2 Machine stitch round the edge of the needlepoint, leaving a small gap for turning. Trim the canvas to 1cm (¹/₂in) and the fabric to 1·5cm (⁵/₈in). Trim across the corners to reduce bulk and turn the cover right sides out.
3 Cut 30cm (12in) lengths of wool in different colours and attach to both ends of the cushion to make a fringe (see pages 121–2). Use threads to match the needlepoint, and attach a length under every second stitch. Knot the strands together to make a net fringe. Insert the cushion pad.

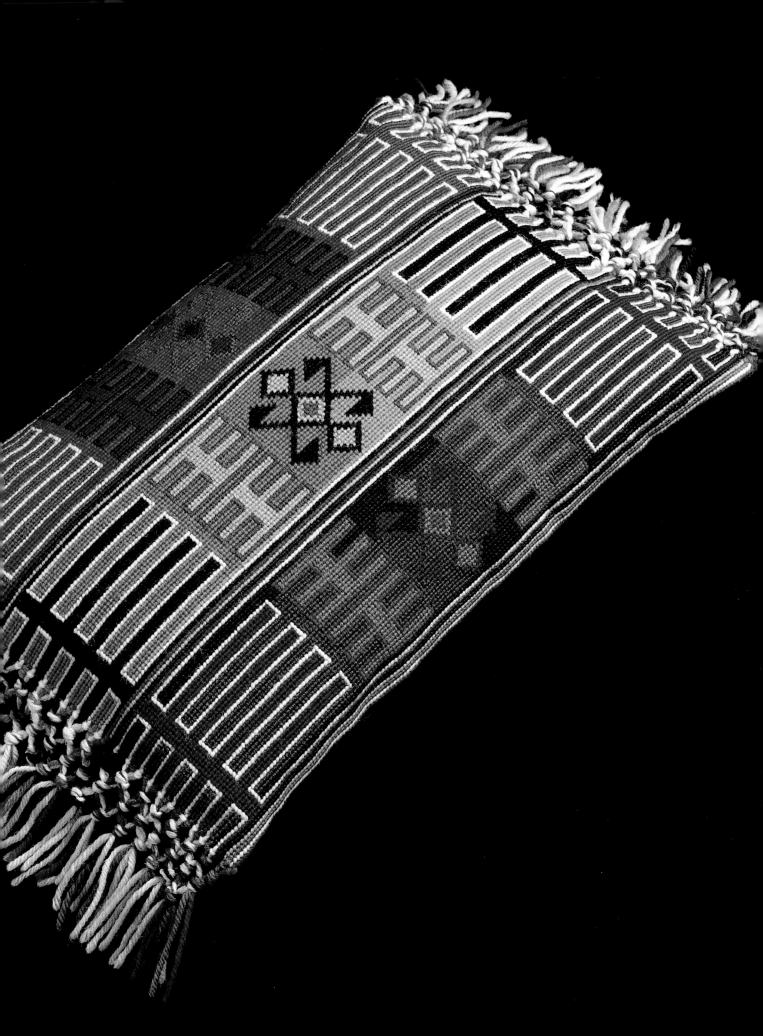

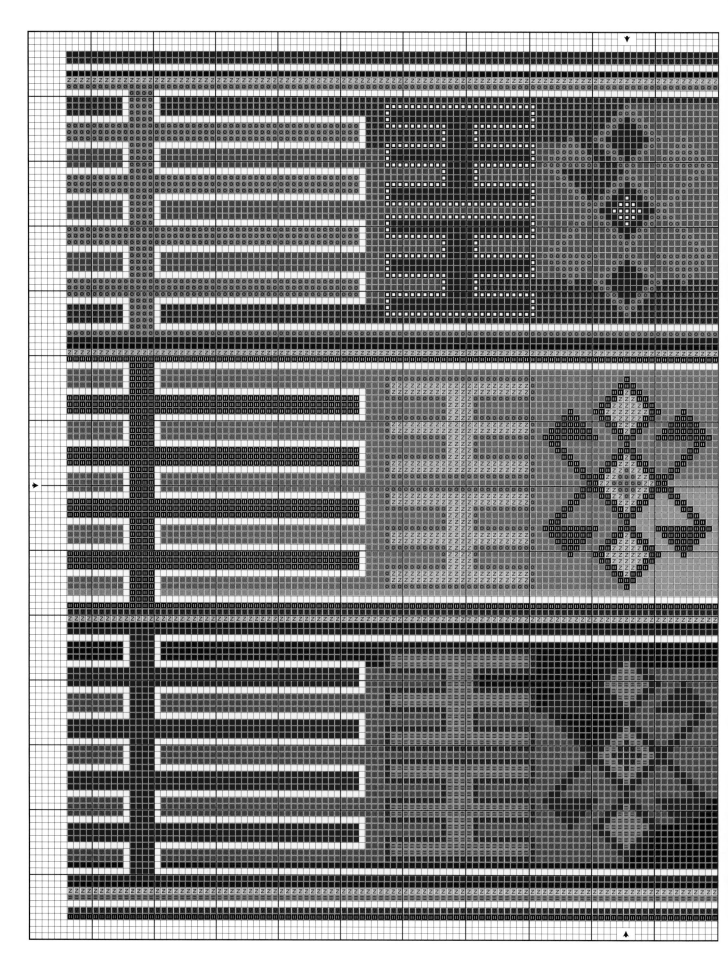

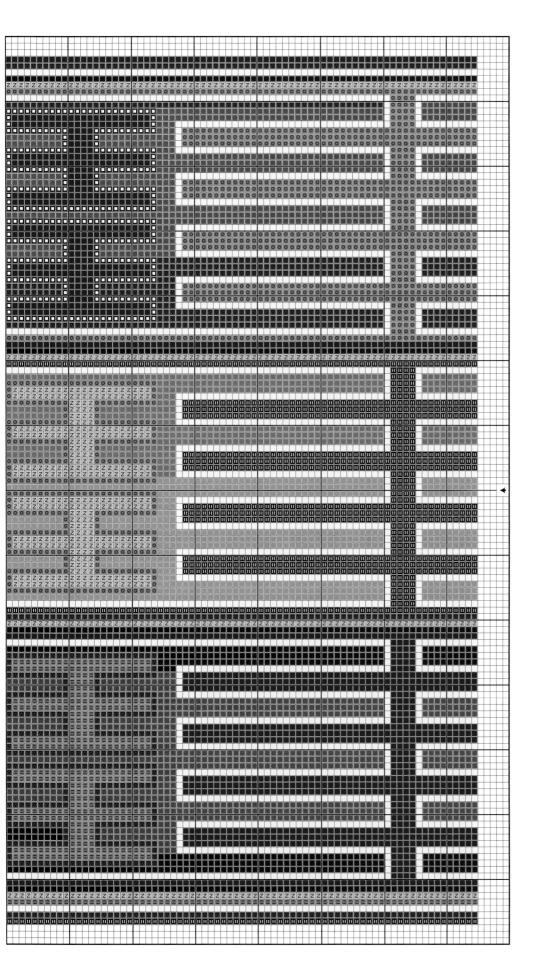

◯ Anchor 8836
▢ Anchor 8838
𝗜𝗜 Anchor 8840
‒ Anchor 8900
Anchor 8902
Anchor 8904
Z Anchor 9508
Anchor 9510
Anchor 9512
Anchor 8032
Anchor 8238
▽ Anchor 8240
Anchor 8242

Afyon Neck Purse

Afyon in western Anatolia was formerly called Afyonkarahisar ('the Dark Opium Castle'), and the people of this area continue to cultivate the opium poppy, for medicinal purposes. The Anatolian kilims often have evil-eye (nazarlik) symbols to protect their owners against injury or misfortune, and a central ram's-horn motif (koçboynuzu) is common. This neck purse was inspired by a design on a flat woven bag used to hold the ends of tent poles during travel. Like the Khorasan bags, the original has a variegated effect produced by variations in the dyes, and the design echoes this by mixing different coloured threads in the needle.

Image size: 57 x 90 stitches, 10·3 x 16·3cm (4¹/₈ x 6³/₈in)

MATERIALS

....

two pieces of 14-count canvas, each 15 x 23cm (6 x 9in)
Appleton crewel wool:
  4 skeins of 983
  2 skeins of 321, 323, 692, 992, 993, 205, 207, 988
size 22 tapestry needle
15 x 50cm (6 x 20in) of lightweight cotton lining fabric
scissors
pins
matching sewing thread
bone beads to decorate (optional)

....

TO STITCH

Before stitching, it is advisable to read the sections 'Materials and Equipment' and 'Techniques'. Begin stitching in one corner, 2·5cm (1in) from the edge. Work the needlepoint in tent stitch, using three strands of crewel wool, and following the chart (right). Stitch across the design from left to right, or vice versa, to produce the desired variegated effect.

Where the chart indicates two colours together, use two strands of one colour and one strand of the second colour (reverse the colours every time you start a new length, to produce a variegated effect). Stitch two identical panels to form the front and back of the purse. Once the stitching is complete, stretch the needlepoint, as shown on pages 116–17.

TO MAKE UP

1 Cut two pieces of the lining fabric the same size as the canvas front and back. Pin one lining piece to each canvas piece, right sides together. Machine stitch close to the edge of the needlepoint, leaving a gap down one side for turning.

2 On each piece, trim the seam allowance to 1cm (¹/₂in), cut across the corners to reduce bulk and turn right sides out. Slipstitch the gap closed. Press on the reverse side.

3 Pin front and back sections together, wrong sides facing. Oversew the sides together, using two strands of crewel wool.

4 Using several lengths of black crewel wool, make two plaited cords (see page 123) long enough to form a strap that extends to the centre bottom of the purse. Pin the strap in position, leaving 5cm (2in) ends hanging down at the bottom, and stitch the plaited cord securely to the sides of the purse. Thread two or three bone beads onto each side of the strap, and tie together at the top. Wrap the strap in different colours (see page 123). Make some simple tassels (see pages 123–4) and sew them securely to the sides. To finish, add bone beads to short lengths of plaited wool and attach these to the bag by wrapping.

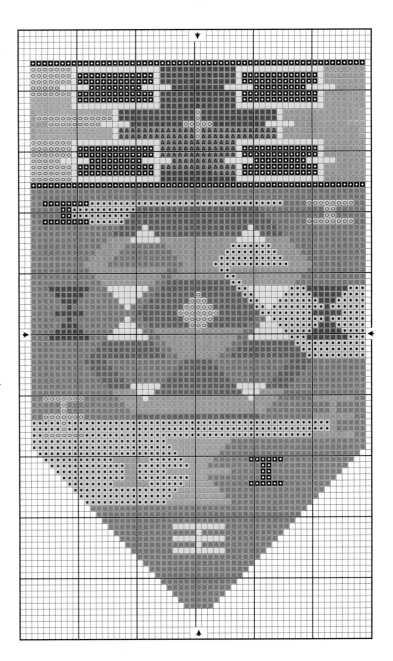

KEY

▨	Appleton 321
▨	Appleton 323
○	Appleton 692
▨	Appleton 321 + 692
◆	Appleton 993
□	Appleton 992
▨	Appleton 207
▨	Appleton 205
△	Appleton 205 + 207
▨	Appleton 983
▪	Appleton 988 + 983

Balikesir Cushion

Nomadic people transport all their belongings in bags, furniture being somewhat impractical. So, their bags are made in many shapes and sizes to accommodate different possessions, such as clothing, bedding and household items. The simple evil-eye (nazarlik) is a common motif on these bags. Çuval are large square bags for carrying clothing. In the yurt, they double up as cushions or pillows, so they provide highly appropriate inspiration for this cushion.

Image size: 190 x 198 stitches, 40·2 x 42·4cm (15⁷/₈ x 16³/₄in)

MATERIALS

50 x 55cm (20 x 22in) of
   12-count canvas
Anchor tapestry wool:
   13 skeins of 8262
   5 skeins of 8006, 8032, 8264
   3 skeins of 8892, 8904, 9600
   2 skeins of 8040, 8902
   1 skein of 8036, 8038, 8898
size 20 tapestry needle
scissors

50 x 69cm (20 x 27in) of
   medium-weight cotton fabric
pins
tacking thread
matching sewing thread
sewing needle
40cm (16in) cushion pad
4 large tassels (to make your
   own, see page 00)

TO STITCH

Before stitching, it is advisable to read the sections 'Materials and Equipment' and 'Techniques'. Begin stitching in one top corner, 5cm (2in) from the edge. Work the needlepoint in tent stitch, using a single strand of tapestry wool, and following the chart overleaf. When the whole chart has been stitched, turn the chart 180 degrees to stitch the final border (see chart). Once the stitching is complete, stretch the needlepoint, as shown on pages 116–17.

TO MAKE UP

1 Make a 1·5cm (⁵/₈in) hem along both short edges of the cotton fabric. Cut the fabric in half lengthways. With right sides facing, pin one cut edge to the left-hand side of the canvas and the other cut edge to the right-hand edge of the canvas. Overlap the two fabric panels and tack through all layers round the edge of the needlepoint.

2 Machine stitch round the edge of the needlepoint, leaving a small gap for turning. Trim the canvas to 1cm (¹/₂in) and the fabric to 1·5cm (⁵/₈in). Trim across the corners to reduce bulk and turn the cover right sides out.

3 To make the plaited edging, cut forty-eight 61cm (24in) lengths of off-white wool. Group these into four bundles of twelve lengths each. Plait each bundle, to make four plaited cords. Stitch these plaited cords along the edges of the cushion, matching the centres of the cords to the centres of the sides, and leaving the ends hanging down at the corners of the cushion.

4 At each corner, wrap together the two plaited cords using a contrasting colour (see page 123). Then unravel the ends of the plaited cords, re-group these threads into four bundles and plait into four small cords. Wrap the ends of the small plaited cords using a contrasting colour. Trim neatly.

5 Insert the cushion pad.

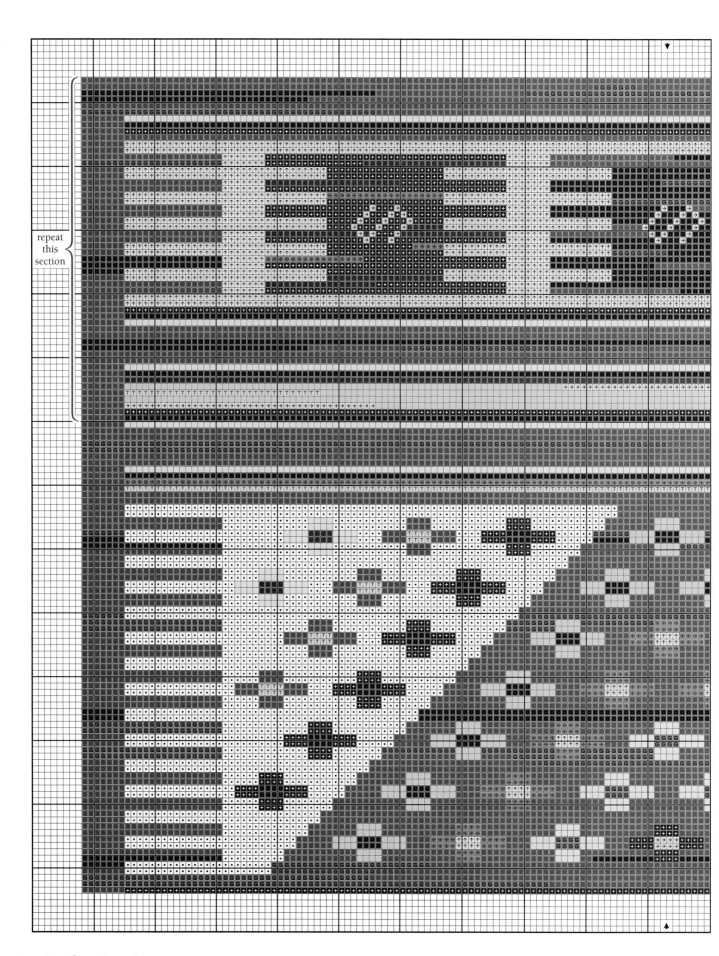

repeat this section

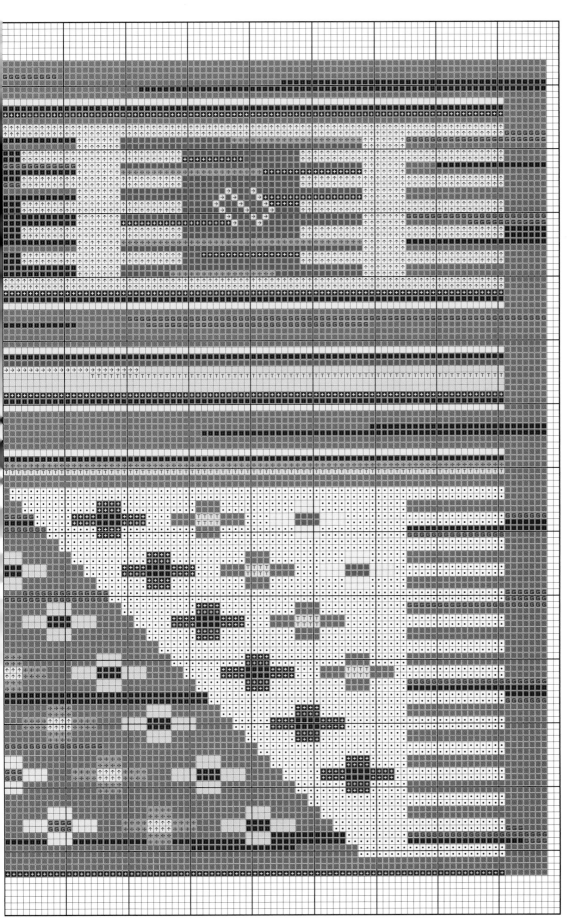

·I·	Anchor 8898
▓	Anchor 8902
✚	Anchor 8904
☐	Anchor 8892
→	Anchor 8036
T	Anchor 8038
☐	Anchor 8040
▒	Anchor 8262
▥	Anchor 8264
G	Anchor 9600
•	Anchor 8032
↑	Anchor 8006

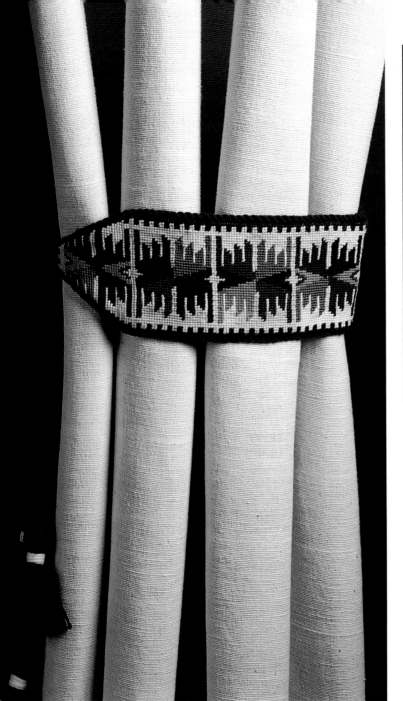

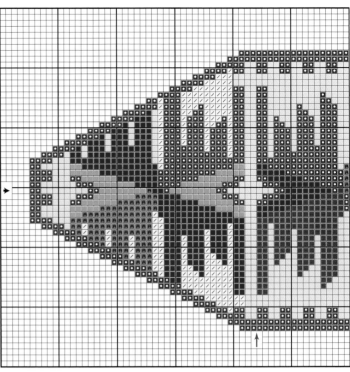

Adana
Curtain Tiebacks

The repeated border design used for our curtain tiebacks is probably the elibelinde motif from the Adana region. This is a mother goddess figure, the symbol of life and birth, with a symbolic baby. As here, this motif often appears with a mirror image.

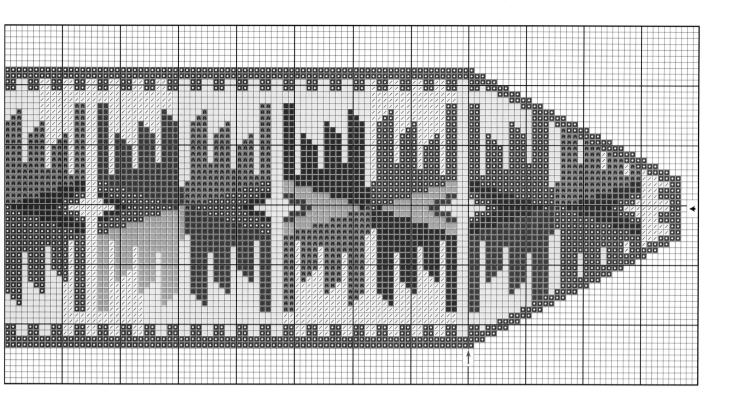

TO STITCH

The chart consists of two shaped ends with a 20cm (8in) repeat in the centre. To make a 58cm (23in) tieback, repeat the centre section twice. Repeating the centre section three times makes a 76cm (30in) tieback, suitable for heavyweight curtains.

Before stitching, it is advisable to read the sections 'Materials and Equipment' and 'Techniques'. Fold the canvas in half lengthways and tack along the fold, to make a guide line. Begin stitching 4cm (1½in) from one end. Work an end panel in tent stitch, using a single strand of tapestry wool, and following the chart above.

Work two repeats of the centre section, then the other end panel. If you require a pair of tiebacks, work the second one to match. Once the stitching is complete, stretch the needlepoint, as shown on pages 116–17.

TO MAKE UP

1 Trim the excess canvas to 1cm (½in). Snip into the corners, fold the excess to the reverse side and tack in place.
2 Place the tieback on the interfacing and draw round the outline. Cut just inside the outline. Iron the interfacing to the reverse side of the cotton fabric. Trim the fabric to 1cm (½in), fold the excess over onto the interfacing, and tack in place.
3 Place tieback and fabric backing together, wrong sides facing. Slipstitch together round the edge.
4 Cut the cord in half and pin one piece to each side of the tieback, centring the cord and leaving the long ends hanging at each end. Stitch the cord invisibly, but securely, to the edge of the tieback.

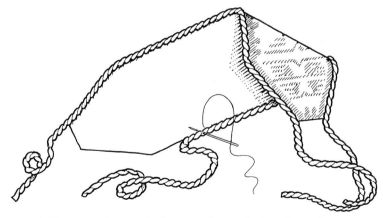

5 Fit a tassel over the knot at the end of each cord (see page 124). Wrap the tieback round the curtain, and tie the cord loosely (to a hook, if preferred), leaving the tassels to hang down at the side.

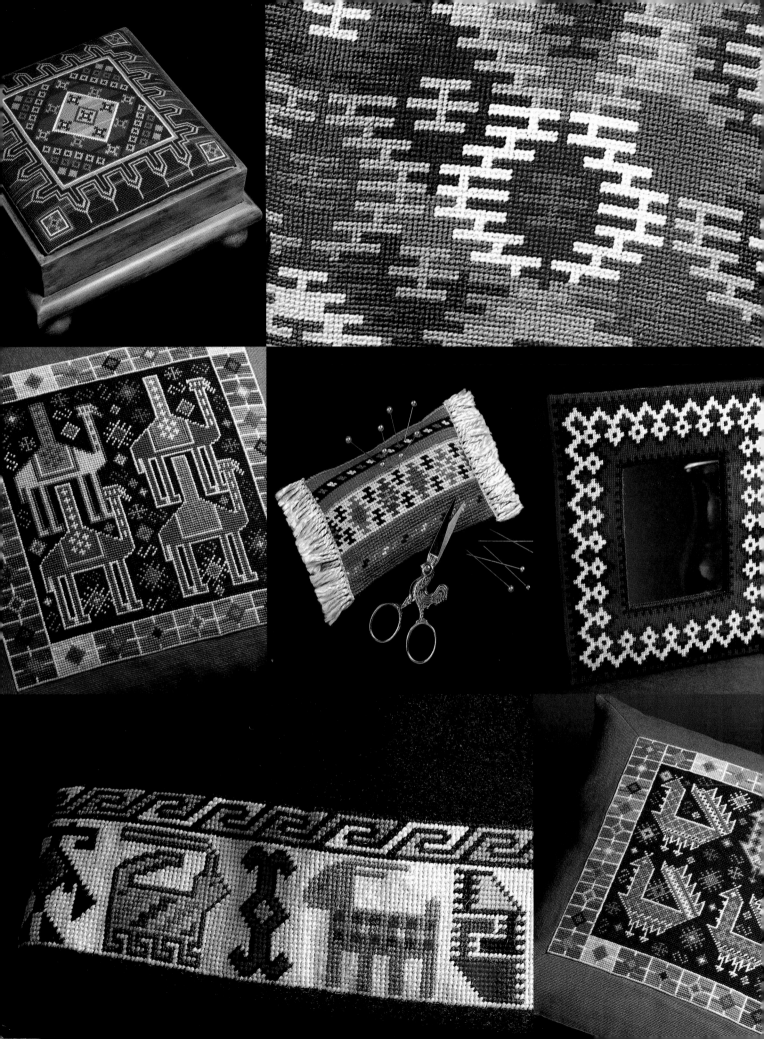

DESIGNS FROM
Persia

....

For many years, in the West, kilims were seen as
inferior to knotted 'oriental' carpets. Kilims were even
used as protective covers for Persian carpets during
their transportation to western markets. Then, in the
early sixties, enthusiasts became aware of the strong
colours and wonderful geometric designs in Qashqai
kilims, and soon kilims became very fashionable
in the West, as wallhangings and objets d'art.

Persia (Iran) is home to a tremendous number
of peoples, with widely differing origins, and the
kilim traditions reflect this diversity.
The exquisitely-detailed animal motifs of the
Shahsavan kilims are quite unlike the rich banded
designs of Saveh kilims, or the dazzling all-over
patterns of Veramin kilims – giving us a wealth
of designs to adapt to needlepoint.

....

Shahsavan Camel Cushion

The Shahsavan people weave delightful and highly complex designs, such as the camel surrounded by small symbolic motifs that has been adapted to make our cushion. The camel is central to the existence of many nomadic peoples, as a means of transport, and a measure of a family's wealth. This design looks more substantial when 'framed' in matching fabric, as in the cushion, but, if preferred, it could be made into a smaller cushion without the fabric border.

Image size: 145 x 141 stitches, 30·7 x 29·8cm (12^{1}/$_{8}$ x 11^{3}/$_{4}$in)

MATERIALS
....

40cm (16in) square of
  12-count canvas
Anchor tapestry wool:
  6 skeins of 9798
  4 skeins of 8006
  2 skeins of 8054, 8262,
    8898, 8900, 9016, 9020,
    9636, 9678
  1 skein of 8036, 8260

size 20 tapestry needle
scissors
50 x 115cm (20 x 45in) of
  medium-weight cotton fabric
pins
tacking thread
matching sewing thread
sewing needle
45cm (18in) cushion pad

....

TO STITCH
....

Before stitching, it is advisable to read the sections 'Materials and Equipment' and 'Techniques'. Begin stitching 5cm (2in) from the edge in one of the top corners. Work the needlepoint in tent stitch, using a single strand of tapestry wool, and following the chart overleaf. Work the border first, then the motifs and, finally, fill in the grey background. Once the stitching is complete, stretch the needlepoint, as shown on pages 116–17.

TO MAKE UP
....

1 Cut four 11 x 49cm (4^{1}/$_{4}$ x 19^{1}/$_{4}$in) strips of cotton fabric to make the frame round the needlepoint. Join the strips at the four corners, making diagonal seams, so the frame fits the needlepoint, and leaving a seam allowance round the inside of the 'frame'.
2 Press the seams open. Pin the 'frame' round the needlepoint, one edge at a time (see page 118). Machine stitch the seams.
3 Make a 1·5cm (⁵/₈in) hem along both short edges of the cotton fabric. Cut the fabric in half lengthways. With right sides facing, pin one cut edge to the left-hand side of the canvas and the other cut edge to the right-hand edge of the canvas. Overlap the two fabric panels and tack through all layers round the edge of the needlepoint.
4 Machine stitch round the edge of the cushion cover, using a 1·5cm (1in) seam allowance, and leaving a small gap for turning. Trim across the corners to reduce bulk and turn the cover right sides out.
5 Press the finished cushion cover on the reverse side. Insert the cushion pad.

KEY

- Anchor 8262
- Anchor 8260
- Anchor 9678
- Anchor 9636
- Anchor 9020
- Anchor 9016
- Anchor 8054
- Anchor 8036
- Anchor 8006
- Anchor 9798
- Anchor 8900
- Anchor 8898

Shahsavan Peacock Cushion

Kilims are a form of visual communication, illustrating the hopes and desires of the weavers through their motifs and symbols. The patterns and motifs have been handed down through the generations, but some meanings have been lost over time. To the Shahsavan, the peacock is a symbol of good luck, the star expresses happiness, and the 's' is a fertility symbol. As with the Shahsavan Camel Cushion, this design looks more substantial when 'framed' in matching fabric, as here, but it could be made into a smaller cushion without the fabric border.

Image size: 145 x 141 stitches, 30·7 x 29·8cm (12¹/₈ x 11³/₄in)

MATERIALS

40cm (16in) square of
  12-count canvas
Anchor tapestry wool:
  7 skeins of 9798
  3 skeins of 8006
  2 skeins of 8054, 8262,
    8900, 9020, 9636
  1 skein of 8036, 8260, 8898,
    9016, 9678

size 20 tapestry needle
scissors
50 x 115cm (20 x 45in) of
    medium-weight cotton fabric
pins
tacking thread
matching sewing thread
sewing needle
45cm (18in) cushion pad

TO STITCH

Before stitching, it is advisable to read the sections 'Materials and Equipment' and 'Techniques'. Begin stitching 5cm (2in) from the edge in one of the top corners. Work the needlepoint in tent stitch, using a single strand of tapestry wool, and following the chart overleaf. Work the border first, then the motifs and, finally, fill in the grey background. Once the stitching is complete, stretch the needlepoint, as shown on pages 116–17.

TO MAKE UP

1 Cut four 11 x 49cm (4¹/₄ x 19¹/₄in) strips of cotton fabric to make the frame round the needlepoint. Join the strips at the four corners, making diagonal seams, so the frame fits the needlepoint, and leaving a seam allowance round the inside of the 'frame'.
2 Press the seams open. Pin the 'frame' round the needlepoint, one edge at a time (see page 118). Machine stitch the seams.
3 Make a 1·5cm (⁵/₈in) hem along both short edges of the cotton fabric. Cut the fabric in half lengthways. With right sides facing, pin one cut edge to the left-hand side of the canvas and the other cut edge to the right-hand edge of the canvas. Overlap the two fabric panels and tack through all layers round the edge of the needlepoint.
4 Machine stitch round the edge of the cushion cover, using a 1·5cm (1in) seam allowance, and leaving a small gap for turning. Trim across the corners to reduce bulk and turn the cover right sides out.
5 Press the finished cushion cover on the reverse side. Insert the cushion pad.

Designs from Persia

KEY

- ■ Anchor 8262
- 1 Anchor 8260
- ■ Anchor 9678
- ◇ Anchor 9636
- ■ Anchor 9020
- ✕ Anchor 9016
- ☐ Anchor 8054
- ·. Anchor 8036
- ☐ Anchor 8006
- ◆ Anchor 9798
- ■ Anchor 8900
- ╱ Anchor 8898

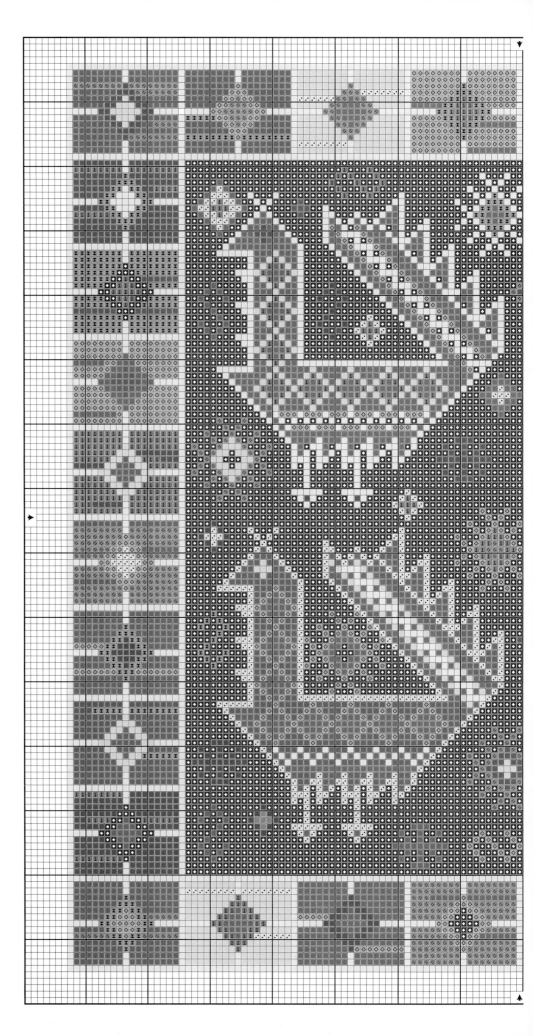

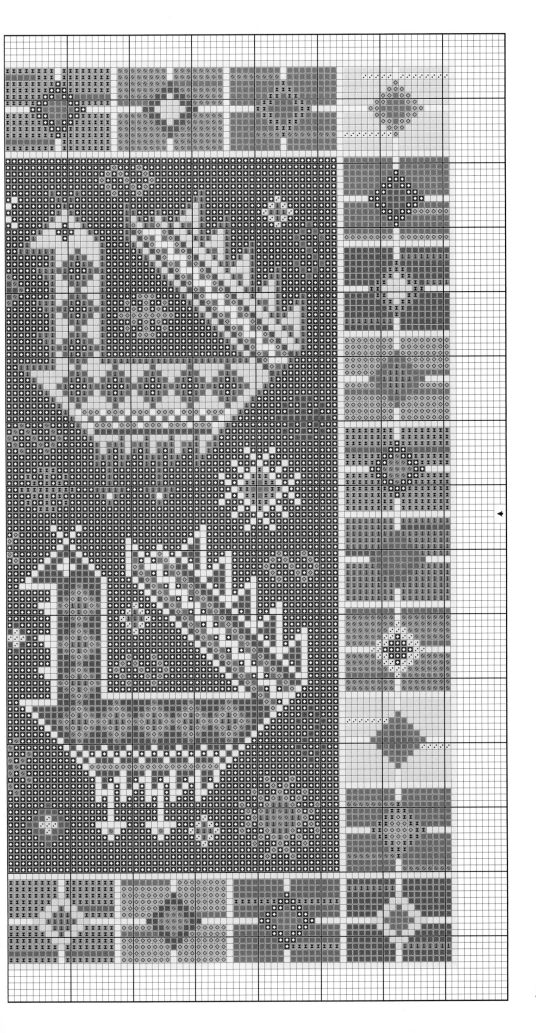

Shirvan Pin Cushion

Shirvan is a prolific rug-making area, with a history of weaving going back to the sixteenth century. The kilims from this area generally have repeat motifs in rows, or an all-over pattern that relies on inspired colour combinations for maximum effect. The crenellated diamond shapes in the design for this delightful pin cushion are typical of Shirvan, but they also appear in Anatolian kilims.

█◄ DMC 355
▐▐ DMC 945
▢ DMC 644
▓ DMC 502
██ DMC 930
██ DMC 898
▣ DMC 310

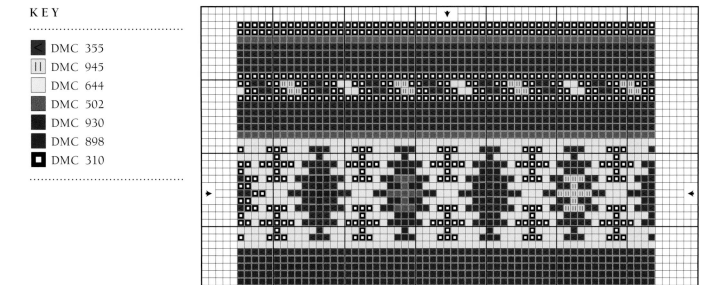

Image size: 47 x 59 stitches, 8·5 x 10·7cm (3³/₈ x 4¹/₄in)

MATERIALS

15 x 18cm (6 x 7in) of
  14-count canvas
DMC coton perlé no. 3:
  1 skein of 310, 355, 502,
    644, 898, 930, 945
size 20 tapestry needle
scissors
15 x 18cm (6 x 7in) of
  medium-weight cotton fabric
pins
matching sewing thread
small amount of polyester
stuffing
sewing needle

TO STITCH

Before stitching, it is advisable to read the sections 'Materials and Equipment' and 'Techniques'. Begin stitching 3cm (1¹/₄in) from the edge. Work the needlepoint in tent stitch, using a single strand of coton perlé, and following the chart above. Once the stitching is complete, stretch the needlepoint, as shown on pages 116–17.

TO MAKE UP

1 Pin the cotton fabric to the needlepoint, right sides facing. Machine stitch round the sides, leaving a gap at one end for turning.
2 Trim the seam allowance to 1cm (¹/₂in) and cut across the corners to reduce bulk. Turn right sides out, and fill the cushion firmly with polyester stuffing. Slipstitch the gap closed.
3 Cut a bundle of 8cm (3in) lengths of 644 coton perlé, and make a fringe at each end of the pin cushion (see pages 121–2).

Bakhtiari Footstool

The Bakhtiari are related to the Lurs, one of the original ethnic groups of Iran, and, until recently, they were isolated from the rest of the world by poor communications. Their kilims were woven entirely for their own use, as floor coverings and functional bags for storage or transportation. The distinctive design used for this footstool was inspired by the kilims woven by the Bakhtiari of Shushstar – these designs often have a central design apparently 'floating' on a plain background.

Image size: 145 x 145 stitches, 30·7cm (12¹/₈in)

MATERIALS

40cm (16in) square of
   14-count canvas
Anchor tapestry wool:
   8 skeins of 9796
   2 skeins of 8262, 8732, 8734,
     9564, 9566, 9794
   1 skein of 8032, 8040, 8042,
     8264, 9426, 9562, 9790
size 20 tapestry needle
scissors
30cm (12in) footstool
heavyweight staple gun
33cm (13in) square of heavyweight calico

TO STITCH

Before stitching, it is advisable to read the sections 'Materials and Equipment' and 'Techniques'. Work the needlepoint in tent stitch, using a single strand of tapestry wool, and following the chart overleaf. Stitch three-quarters of the design as given on the chart, then turn the chart 180 degrees to stitch the remainder of the design (see page 116). Once the stitching is complete, stretch the needlepoint, as shown on pages 116–17.

TO MAKE UP

1 Position the needlepoint centrally over the footstool pad. Put a staple part way in to the needlepoint, at the centre of each side. Turn the footstool pad over and insert a staple in the centre of one edge. Stretch the needlepoint slightly before putting a staple in the opposite side. Repeat on the other two sides, checking all the time that the needlepoint is square.
2 Insert a staple every 2·5cm (1in) round the edge, mitring the corners neatly. Check again that the needlepoint is square. Cut away the excess canvas.
3 Press under 1·5cm (⁵/₈in) round all edges of the calico. With raw edges to the inside, attach the calico to the underside of the footstool using staples. Drop the covered pad into the footstool and secure with screws.

KEY
....

▢ Anchor 8032
▨ Anchor 8040
☒ Anchor 8042
▨ Anchor 8262
■ Anchor 8264
T Anchor 8732
▨ Anchor 8734
▥ Anchor 9562
▣ Anchor 9564
▨ Anchor 9566
⋮ Anchor 9426
▨ Anchor 9790
D Anchor 9794
◆ Anchor 9796
→ repeat
....

Bijar Tote Bag

Bijar is a market town near the border with Kurdistan (the name literally means 'mixing of people'). The akimbo motif used here, a symbol of motherhood, is typical of this area of north-west Persia, but the border design of small squares is quite unusual. The original kilim has a variegated effect produced by variations in the dyes, so the bag echoes this by mixing different coloured threads in the needle.

Image size: 110 x 110 stitches, 20cm (8in) square

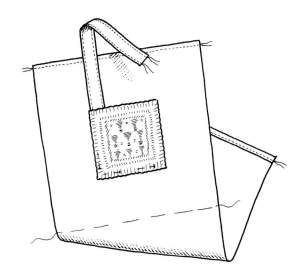

MATERIALS

30 cm (12in) square of 14-count canvas	size 22 tapestry needle
	scissors
Appleton crewel wool:	100 x 90cm (41 x 36in) denim
3 skeins of 321, 323	pins
2 skeins of 471, 473, 503, 862, 865, 992	tacking thread
	matching sewing thread
1 skein of 998	sewing needle

TO STITCH

Before stitching, it is advisable to read the sections 'Materials and Equipment' and 'Techniques'. Begin stitching in one corner, 2·5cm (1in) from the edge. Work the needlepoint in tent stitch, using three strands of crewel wool, and following the chart overleaf. Stitch the border first. Then stitch the central area, working from left to right, or vice versa, to produce the variegated effect that simulates the weave on traditional kilims.

Where the chart indicates two colours together, use two strands of one colour and one strand of the second colour (reverse the colours every time you start a new length, to produce a variegated effect). Once the stitching is complete, stretch the needlepoint, as shown on pages 116–17.

TO MAKE UP

1 Cut a piece of denim 54 x 100cm (21 x 41in). Turn under 5mm (¹/₄in) at each short end of the denim and machine stitch.
2 Trim the excess canvas to 1cm (¹/₂in). Turn the excess canvas to the reverse side and tack.
3 To make the handles, cut a length of denim 12 x 100cm (4³/₄ x 39¹/₂in). Fold it in half lengthways, right sides together. Machine stitch 1cm (¹/₂in) from the raw edges. Turn right sides out, the seam down one edge, and press. Machine stitch two lines, 5mm (¹/₄in) apart, close to each long edge. Cut in half lengthways to make two handles.
4 Fold the rectangle of denim in half lengthways and tack along the fold to mark the bottom edge of the bag.

Place the needlepoint panel centrally on one side of the bag, 10cm (4in) from the stitched edge (the top of the bag), wrong side of canvas to right side of denim. Pin in position.
5 Pin the ends of one handle under the top corners of the needlepoint. Slipstitch round all sides of the needlepoint, attaching it securely to the denim and the handle. On the other side of the bag, attach the other handle, slipstitching it to the denim in the same position.
6 Turn the bag wrong sides out. Machine stitch the side seams. Press the seams flat. Open out the corners and match the centre-bottom fold to the side seams. Stitch across the corners 5cm (2in) from the corner, at right angles to the side seam. Zigzag outside this stitching and trim off the corner. Turn the bag right sides out.

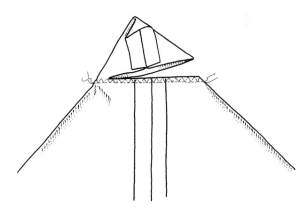

7 Turn under 5cm (2in) along the top edge of the bag, then pin and tack. Without catching the handles in the stitching, work two rows of machine stitching, 5mm (¹/₄in) apart, close to the edge of the hem. Reinforce the handles by machine stitching a double row of stitches 5mm (¹/₄in) apart, in a square, at each end.

KEY

....

■ Appleton 323	■ Appleton 865	■ Appleton 998	▽ Appleton 321 + 323
▲ Appleton 321	■ Appleton 862	□ Appleton 992	⊖ Appleton 471 + 321
○ Appleton 473	■ Appleton 503	■ Appleton 321 + 473	△ Appleton 471 + 473
◇ Appleton 471			

....

Moghan Hat

The Moghan are Shahsavan people who migrate between the shores of
the Caspian sea and Mount Savalon, an area rich in folkloric traditions.
Turkic motifs, such as the double-headed animals, have been woven into
their kilims for centuries. Bridal kilims often have cream backgrounds,
and this provided the inspiration for the cosy hat.

Image size: 330 x 38 stitches, 59·8 x 6·9cm
(23¹/₂ x 2³/₄in)

MATERIALS
....

66 x 13cm (26 x 5in) of
  14-count canvas
Appleton crewel wool:
  5 skeins of 333, 331A, 992
  3 skeins of 998
  2 skeins of 473, 504
  1 skein of 325
size 22 tapestry needle
scissors

35 x 70cm (12 x 27¹/₂in) of
  dark-grey fleecy fabric
pins
tailor's chalk
tacking thread
matching sewing thread
sewing needle
adhesive tape
....

KEY
....

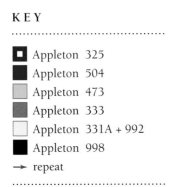

■ (white) Appleton 325
■ Appleton 504
■ Appleton 473
■ Appleton 333
□ Appleton 331A + 992
■ Appleton 998
→ repeat

....

TO STITCH
....

Before stitching, it is advisable to read the sections
'Materials and Equipment' and 'Techniques'. Work the
needlepoint in tent stitch, using three strands of crewel
wool, and following the chart below. Work two repeats
of the chart, to make a narrow band. Where the chart
indicates two colours together, use two strands of one
colour and one strand of the second colour (reverse the
colours every time you start a new length, to produce
a variegated effect). Once the stitching is complete,
stretch the needlepoint, as shown on pages 116–17.

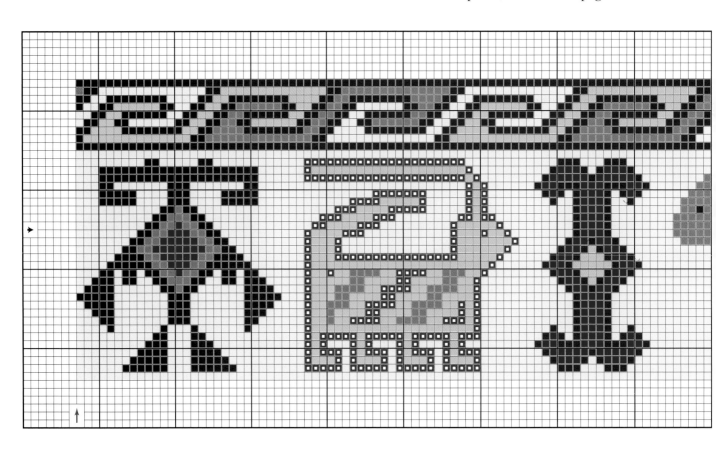

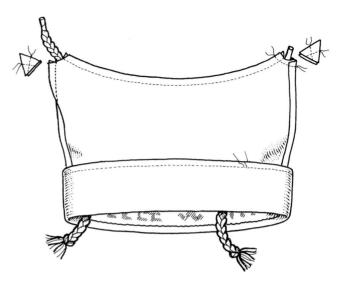

1 Fold the fleecy fabric in half lengthways to make a square. Pin the sides. Draw a curved line along the fold (see diagram), using tailor's chalk, to shape the top of the hat. Cut along the curved line through both layers.

2 Stitch seams along the curved top and down each side. Trim the seams. Turn the bottom edge up to make a 7cm (2³⁄₄in) hem. Machine stitch the hem in place, 5mm (¹⁄₄in) from the top edge.

3 Trim the canvas round the needlepoint to 1cm (¹⁄₂in). With right sides together, pin, then machine stitch, the short ends together. On both long edges, fold the excess canvas to the reverse side and tack.

4 Turn the hat right sides out. Pin and tack the needle-point round the bottom of the hat, matching seams, and leaving a 1cm (¹⁄₂in) border of fabric showing below. Hem the needlepoint to the hat along both edges.

5 Cut thirty 60cm (24in) lengths of black crewel wool, divide into three equal bundles and make a plaited cord (see page 123). Tie a knot at each end of the cord, 5cm (2in) from the end, and wrap a piece of adhesive tape round the middle of the cord. Cut through the centre of the taped area of cord.

6 Turn the points of the hat inside out. Trim across the tops of the points to leave a 5mm (¹⁄₄in) gap, and feed the taped ends of the cord through. Machine stitch across the points to secure. Turn the hat right sides out.

7 Cut one bundle of 15cm (6in) lengths of red crewel wool, and another of yellow. Make tassels to fit over the knots at the end of the cords, wrapping the red tassel with blue wool and the yellow tassel with green (see page 123). Trim the ends of the tassels neatly, and tie the cords together.

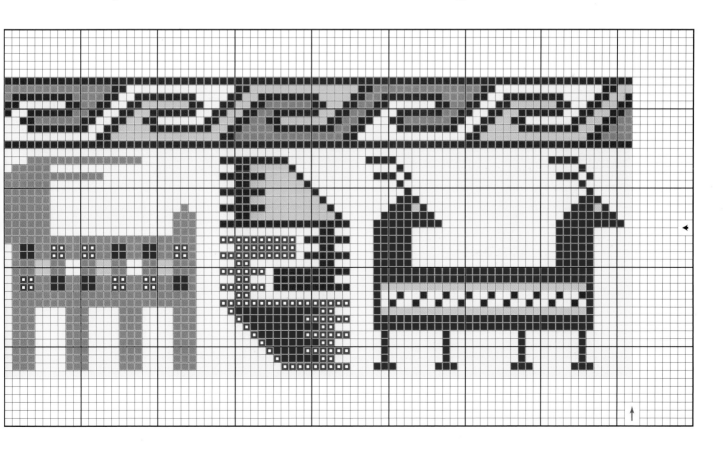

Saveh Letter Holder

The Saveh are semi-nomadic people who live near the Kharaqai mountains. Kilims from this area have intricate horizontal bands, where the space left between the small motifs becomes as important as the motifs themselves. The muted colours of this letter-holder are typical of Saveh kilims, but, in this design they have been highlighted by the inclusion of off-white. The çengel or hook motif protects against evil, and the complex star motifs symbolize happiness.

Image size: 115 x 170 stitches, 20·9 x 30·9cm (8¹/₄ x 12¹/₂in)

MATERIALS

30 x 50cm (12 x 20in) of   scissors
  14-count canvas   25 x 35cm (10 x 14in) cotton
Appleton crewel wool: poplin fabric
  4 skeins of 988, 998   pins
  2 skeins of 207, 209, 321,   tacking thread
    325, 327   matching sewing thread
  1 skein of 205, 323, 692, 841   sewing needle
size 22 tapestry needle

TO STITCH

Before stitching, it is advisable to read the sections 'Materials and Equipment' and 'Techniques'. Work the needlepoint in tent stitch, using three strands of crewel wool, and following the chart overleaf. Work the three sections of the chart leaving at least 2·5cm (1in) of bare canvas between each one. Once the stitching is complete, stretch the needlepoint, as shown on pages 116–17.

TO MAKE UP

1 Cut out the needlepoint pieces leaving a 1·5cm (⁵/₈in) seam allowance around all edges. Cut one piece of cotton poplin 24 x 13cm (9¹/₂ x 5in), one piece 24 x 23cm (9¹/₂ x 9in) and one piece 24 x 35cm (9¹/₂ x 14in).

2 Pin the bottom needlepoint panel to the smallest piece of cotton poplin, right sides together, and machine stitch together along the top edge. Stitch the central needlepoint panel to the medium-size piece of cotton poplin in the same way. Trim the stitched seam allowances to 5mm (¹/₄in). Turn right sides out.

3 Pin the top needlepoint panel to one end of the large piece of cotton poplin, right sides together, with the point of the needlepoint panel 5mm (¹/₄in) from the edge of the fabric. Machine stitch the two layers together along both top edges of the triangle. Trim the seam allowance to 5mm (¹/₄in), trim across the top corner, and turn right sides out.

4 On the two smallest panels, turn under the bottom edges of the canvas, and slipstitch to the cotton poplin. Press all the pieces on the reverse side.

5 Layer the three sections together, right sides up, to form the letter rack, with the largest piece at the bottom. Tack through all layers along the sides. Machine stitch down the sides 5mm (¹/₄in) away from the edge of the needlepoint. Trim the seam allowance to 3mm (¹/₈in), remove the tacking and turn the bottom two sections to the reverse side. Ease out the seams and corners and press. Stitch along the sides 5mm (¹/₄in) from the edge. Reinforce the seams by stitching over them again. Trim across the bottom corners and turn right sides out.

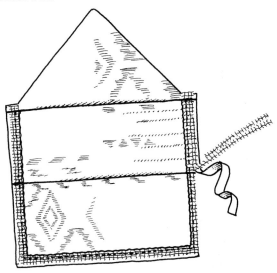

6 Make a plaited cord to fit round the edge of the letter holder (see page 123). Fold it in half and tie a knot to make a small loop in the middle for hanging the letter rack. Stitch the plait to the side edges of the letter holder, leaving the ends to hang down. Make some tassels to decorate the sides and bottom edge (see pages 123–4). Stitch the tassels securely in place.

KEY

 Appleton 998	 Appleton 841	 Appleton 325	 Appleton 207
• Appleton 988	Appleton 321	Appleton 327	Appleton 209
▽ Appleton 692	Appleton 323	Appleton 205	

Saveh Letter Holder　103

Qashqai Mirror Frame

Women have a high standing in Qashqai culture, and they maintain a strong influence in the home. Their freedom is evident in the boldness of colour and pleasing geometry of their kilims. The design for this mirror frame is adapted from a traditional Qashqai border pattern.

Image size: 122 x 134 stitches, 22·1 x 24·3cm (8³/₄ x 9⁵/₈in)

MATERIALS

28 x 30cm (11 x 12in) of 14-count canvas

Appleton crewel wool:
4 skeins of 992
3 skeins of 993, 998
2 skeins of 326, 328, 504, 505

size 22 tapestry needle

scissors

22 x 25cm (9 x 10in) of foamcore mounting board

12 x 15cm (5 x 6in) mirror tile

double-sided tape

black permanent-ink pen

25 x 90cm (10 x 36in) of black cotton poplin

pins

tacking thread

matching sewing thread

sewing needle

2 small brass rings

TO STITCH

Before stitching, it is advisable to read the sections 'Materials and Equipment' and 'Techniques'. Begin stitching 3cm (1¹/₄in) from the edge of the canvas. Work the needlepoint in tent stitch, using three strands of crewel wool, and following the chart overleaf. Once the stitching is complete, stretch the needlepoint, as shown on pages 116–17.

TO MAKE UP

1 Measure the exact size of the stretched needlepoint, and trim the foamcore mounting board to the same size. Stick the mirror tile in the centre of the foamcore using double-sided tape.

2 Snip into the excess canvas in the centre 'window'. Make diagonal cuts right to the corners of the needlepoint. Trim this excess canvas to 1cm (¹/₂in), turn it under and stick it to the back of the canvas using double-sided tape. Using black permanent ink or a felt pen, colour the first 5mm (¹/₄in) of canvas on the inside of the frame. Leave to dry.

3 Cut four 2·5cm x 28cm (1 x 11in) strips of cotton poplin. Pin these to the outside edges of the canvas, right sides together. Machine stitch together down each side close to the edge of the needlepoint. Trim the canvas to 5mm (¹/₄in).

4 Stick double-sided tape round the inner edges of the needlepoint, on the back, 5mm (¹/₄in) from the edges. Position the needlepoint round the mirror, aligning it with the foamcore. Press firmly to stick the frame to the foamcore.

5 Stick double-sided tape to the back of the foamcore. Trim the short edges of the cotton poplin strips to 5mm (¹/₄in) and fold the cotton poplin over the foamcore, mitring the corners. Stick down neatly on the back.

6 Cut a piece of cotton poplin to cover the back, adding a small seam allowance all round. Press the seam allowance to the reverse side. Pin, tack and hem neatly to the back of the mount. Stitch two small brass rings to the backing fabric for hanging the mirror.

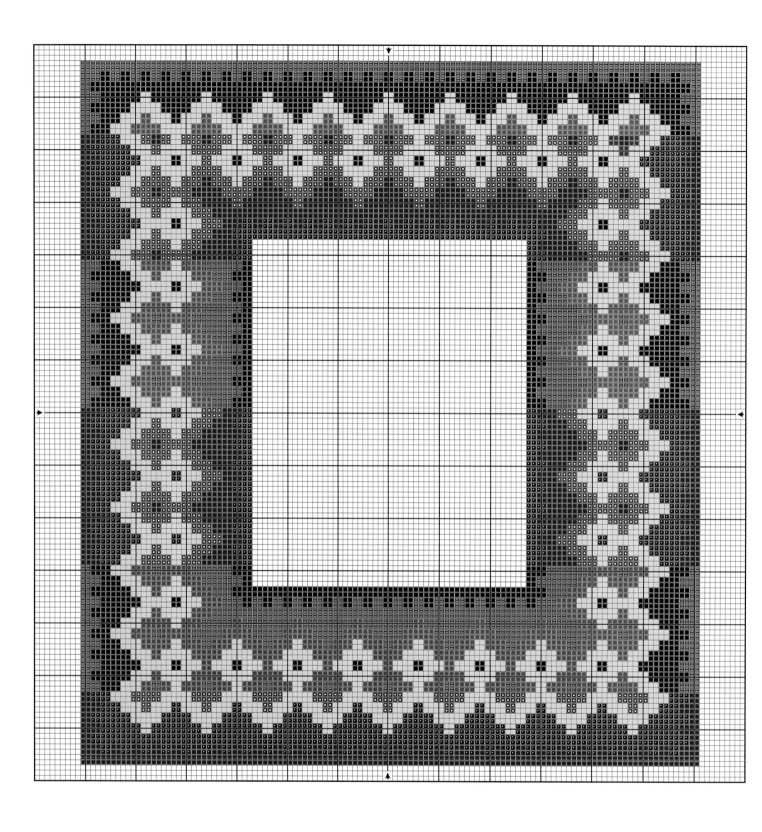

KEY

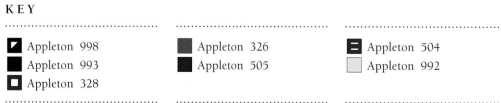

◥ Appleton 998	◼ Appleton 326	⊟ Appleton 504	
◼ Appleton 993	◼ Appleton 505	▢ Appleton 992	
▣ Appleton 328			

Veramin Covered Chair

Banished from their original mountainous home lands, groups of Shahsavan
live in many of the villages around Veramin. The kilims from this area are
generally uncomplicated, boldly geometric designs with attractive, if somewhat

sombre, colours. Gaudy 'eye-dazzler' designs are also common locally. The design for the covered chair combines the two traditions. Its repeating pattern makes it easy to adapt to any size of chair, or perhaps a chair cushion. To cover a large chair seat and back, like the one shown, you will need two hanks of each colour.

MATERIALS

8-count canvas to fit chosen chair (see below)
Appleton tapestry wool:
   121, 926, 125, 151, 882, 924, 967, 153, 155, 961, 964, 126, 922
chair
size 18 tapestry needle

TO STITCH

Before stitching, it is advisable to read the sections 'Materials and Equipment' and 'Techniques'. Measure the size of your chair seat and back and add at least 10cm (4in) to both pieces of canvas to allow for stretching. Fold the canvas in four and mark the centre point. Mark on the canvas the outline of the area of needlepoint required.

   Begin stitching in the centre of the canvas. Work the needlepoint in tent stitch, using two strands of tapestry wool, and following the chart (right). Repeat the pattern as necessary. The design repeats on all sides, so, when you reach the edge of the chart, follow the design from the opposite edge, and, when you reach the bottom of the chart, continue by working from the top of the chart. Once the stitching is complete, stretch the needlepoint, as shown on pages 116–17.

TO MAKE UP

Making up the covered chair will require upholstery techniques, which will depend on the construction of your chosen chair. We recommend that you seek a professional upholsterer, to ensure a successful result.

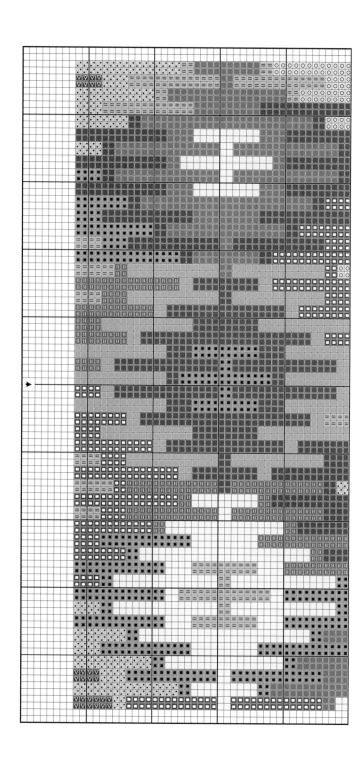

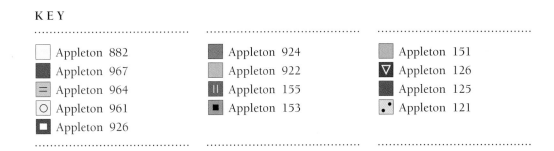

☐ Appleton 882

■ Appleton 967

= Appleton 964

Ⓞ Appleton 961

▣ Appleton 926

■ Appleton 924

☐ Appleton 922

∥ Appleton 155

■ Appleton 153

☐ Appleton 151

▽ Appleton 126

■ Appleton 125

•˙ Appleton 121

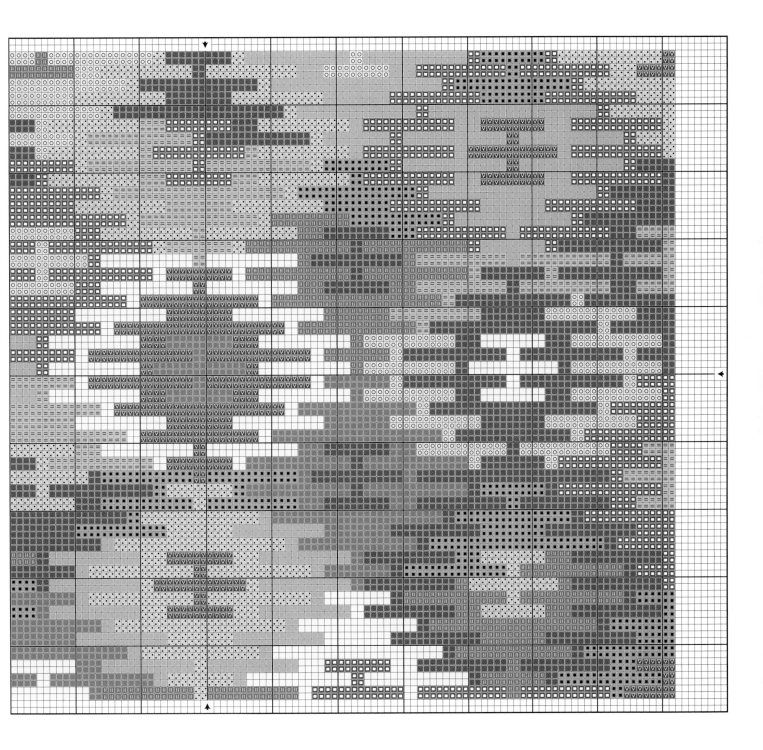

Materials
&
Techniques

Materials and Equipment

YARN

The standard yarn used for needlepoint is definitely wool. Wool is strong and easy to work with, giving excellent coverage of the canvas. Woollen yarn makes the stitched needlepoint extremely durable, and, therefore, suitable for upholstered chairs, cushions and bags. Needlepoint stitched in woollen yarn also has the ability to 'wear clean', so that the article should need no more than an occasional light brushing or tapping to remove dust.

There are two standard woollen yarns used in this book: tapestry and crewel wool. Tapestry wool is similar to double-knitting wool. A single strand is used to cover a 10- or 12-count canvas, and two strands are used to cover a 7- or 8-count canvas.

Crewel wool is much finer than tapestry wool. Three strands are used to cover a 14-count canvas. One of the advantages of working with crewel wool is that the colours can be mixed 'in the needle'. Two similar shades of the same colour produce another shade, whereas two contrasting shades or colours produce an attractive mottled appearance. This technique has been used several times to simulate the striking variations between dye lots found in traditional kilims.

Coton perlé is an alternative cotton yarn that has an attractive sheen. Two strands of no. 5 or a single strand of no. 3 covers a 14-count canvas. Coton perlé is not as hard wearing as wool, but it is suitable for smaller projects, such as the pin cushion (page 88) or book cover (page 28).

The various brands of tapestry and crewel wool have slightly different thicknesses. For example, Appleton tapestry wool is slightly finer than Anchor, so Appleton will not cover a 10-count canvas completely, although the Anchor wool does. Whichever yarn you use, stitch a small sample square to check your tension and the covering ability of the yarn. If necessary, adjust the count size of the canvas accordingly. The yarn should pass through the holes in the canvas easily, but still cover the canvas threads completely. Yarn that is too thick will distort the canvas and eventually fray.

The quantity of yarn used in each project depends on several things: the length of yarn used, how tightly you stitch, and the type of stitch used. Continental tent stitch uses more wool than half-cross stitch (see page 114). In the main, the projects have been stitched in half-cross stitch, therefore, if you prefer to work continental tent stitch, you may need more yarn. One of the delightful features of kilims is the variation between dye lots. Generally in needlepoint, it is preferable to keep to the same dye lots, but, this is not essential here, and variety could even add an extra feature to the design. Nevertheless, buy wool from the same dye lot if you want the design to turn out exactly as shown.

For those who have difficulty obtaining Appleton yarn, a conversion table (page 125) gives the nearest shade in DMC crewel wool. Using an alternative yarn may alter the final appearance because the colour match is not always exact.

CANVAS

There are three types of canvas used for needlepoint: single (mono) canvas, double-thread (Penelope) canvas or interlock canvas. Single canvas woven with a plain weave, uses single threads for the warp and weft. Double-thread canvas woven in a similar way has threads grouped in pairs. Interlock canvas has a warp intertwined round the weft threads to stabilize the weave. This helps to keep the tension even and prevents the canvas from fraying round the edge.

The type you use depends very much on personal preference. Interlock canvas is ideal for tent stitch but, unfortunately, it is only available in white. If using white canvas, take great care to ensure that the canvas is completely covered when stitching with darker colours. Single and double-thread canvases are also available in 'antique', that is, a natural brown colour.

Canvas is available in a range of count sizes that relate to the number of threads per inch. 7-count canvas is the coarsest; it is used for large projects, such as large upholstery and rugs. At the other end of the scale, 'petit point' is a fine 22-count canvas that is stitched with fine crewel wool. A single strand of tapestry wool completely covers 10- or 12-count canvas.

NEEDLES

Tapestry needles for working on canvas have large eyes and a blunt point. The blunt point prevents the canvas from being split and weakened while stitching. The most suitable needle for any piece of work will have an eye large enough to thread the yarn easily, but not so big that the yarn slips through while stitching. The needle and wool must also pass through the canvas without distorting it. Tapestry needles come in sizes 13 to 26, with the larger sizes having smaller numbers. A size 18 needle is ideal for 10- to 12-count canvas.

FRAMES

All the projects in this book are in tent stitch or half-cross stitch. This is a diagonal stitch that distorts the canvas if the stitching is worked in your hand, or with a tight stitch tension. A square cushion can become almost diamond shaped by the time the stitching is complete. To prevent this happening, it is advisable to stretch the canvas on a frame for working. There are several different types of frame. The most suitable for needlepoint has two rotating bars to which you attach the canvas. Rotate the bars to tighten the canvas or move it up or down, to expose the area you are working on. Luxury floor-standing frames are quite expensive, but basic rotating frames are available from needlecraft shops at a very reasonable price. Buy a frame that is wide enough to hold the canvas of your project, remembering that there is extra canvas round all projects. For example: a 45cm (18in) cushion will fit comfortably on a 64cm (25in) frame.

Nevertheless, it is personal preference that determines whether or not you use a frame. Stitches worked on a frame are generally more even, and the canvas is less likely to distort. Working on a frame leaves both hands free, and makes it easier to work quite quickly, taking the needle through the canvas by passing it from one hand to the other. However, needlepoint is more easily transported when not worked on a frame, so you can work in different situations. Unfortunately, it can be tiring and uncomfortable to hold bulky canvas in one hand while you stitch with the other. Embroidery hoops are unsuitable for needlepoint, as the canvas is easily damaged by the rings.

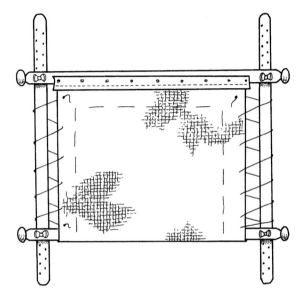

PREPARING THE CANVAS

The canvas measurements given in the instructions for each project include an allowance of excess canvas round the design. The width of this varies from 2·5cm (1in) for small pieces to 8cm (3in) for larger pieces. This excess is needed for mounting the canvas on a frame, and for stretching the finished needlepoint. The making-up instructions with each project explain when to trim away the excess canvas, and by how much.

When working from a chart, count one thread of canvas for each square of the chart and mark out the finished outline of the project with tacking thread. Do not use pencil, as this will make the yarn grubby. If you prefer to begin in the middle of the design, stitch additional tacking lines across the centre of the canvas in both directions. Mount the canvas in the frame as shown above or tape the edges of the canvas with masking tape to prevent the canvas catching as you stitch.

Techniques

NEEDLEPOINT STITCHES

There is a wide variety of needlepoint stitches, but, as the projects in this book are intended to simulate the simple, flat weave of the kilim, only tent stitch has been used. Tent stitch is probably the most important of all canvas stitches. It can be worked in several different ways: as half-cross stitch, continental tent stitch or basketweave tent stitch. All three methods produce the same slanting stitch on the right side of the canvas, but they look completely different on the back, and they have distinct properties. You can use different stitching techniques in the same project, but avoid changing between techniques in the same colour area. I generally use half-cross stitch for blocks of colour, and continental tent stitch to give definition to single rows.

Half-cross stitch

This is the simplest stitch to work, and uses the least yarn. It produces a small straight stitch on the back of the canvas, which does not cover the canvas, therefore, the resulting needlepoint is quite light and pliable. However, single stitches and rows, worked in half-cross stitch can be rather flat and indistinct. Better results are achieved using continental tent stitch. Half-cross stitch is suitable for covering large areas, but, as the stitches all pull in one direction, it is preferable to stitch the work in a frame. Use an interlock or double-thread canvas, if possible.

Continental tent stitch

This technique completely covers both sides of the canvas, and therefore uses more yarn than the other methods. It produces long slanting stitches on the back, resulting in a thick, hard-wearing needlepoint that is ideal for upholstery, such as footstools and chair seats. Many of the kilim designs have single horizontal rows in different shades to give the effect of variations in dye colour. Continental tent stitch is especially suitable for working these single rows, because each stitch is clearly defined.

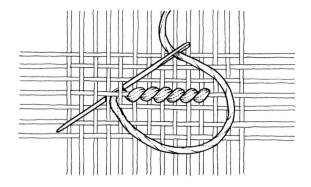

Basketweave tent stitch

This technique is used when covering large areas of background. It is worked on the diagonal, and, on the back, the stitches change direction from horizontal to vertical. Very little distortion occurs because the canvas is pulled in alternate directions by any two adjacent stitches. Any type of canvas can be used with basketweave tent stitch. It may be awkward to use this technique for the designs in this book, as the background areas are often broken up with horizontal shading lines.

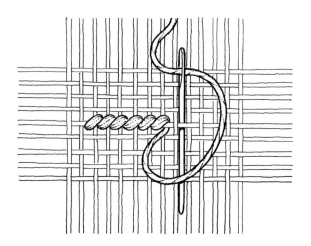

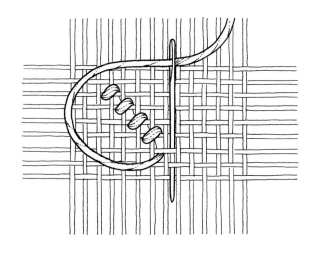

STARTING AND FINISHING

There is no correct place to begin stitching your needlepoint project, although I have given my preference in the project instructions. Some people prefer to start in the middle, and others start in one of the top corners. Wherever you decide to begin, work the motifs first, and leave the background until last.

All the techniques used to work tent stitch begin in the same way. Cut the yarn into 50–60cm (20–24in) lengths. If you work with longer lengths, the yarn will wear thin, not cover the canvas adequately and eventually fray. Make a simple overhand knot at one end of the yarn, and thread your needle with the other end. Take the needle down through the canvas about 2·5cm (1in) from where you want to start stitching, leaving the knot on the right side. As you stitch, the short length of yarn on the reverse side will be caught in the stitches and the knot can be snipped off.

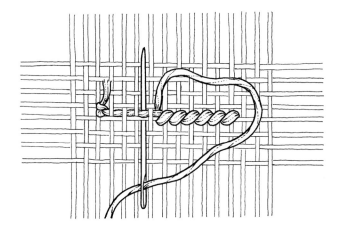

At the end of a length of yarn, either weave the end through the back of five or six stitches, or bring the end up to the right side a short distance away, and trim it once it has been caught in on the back.

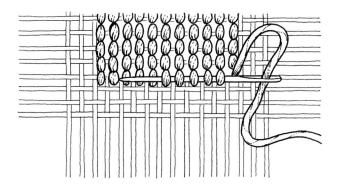

STITCHING

As you stitch, the yarn tends to twist or untwist. If it tends to twist, the yarn will become too thin to cover the canvas. If the yarn becomes untwisted, it is more likely to fray and snap as you stitch. Both problems can be avoided by giving the needle an occasional half-turn, or by letting the needle hang down for a few moments.

The finished needlepoint will also look much better if worked throughout with an even tension. This is achieved by pulling equally on each stitch. If your stitches are too tight, the canvas could be badly distorted and might not be completely covered. If you stitch too loosely, the yarn will tend to loop on the back, and be uneven on the front. The ideal tension produces a soft slanting stitch that completely covers the canvas on the front. This comes with practice, but is easier to achieve when working on a frame.

Unpicking stitches

However carefully you work, sometimes you will find an odd stitch in the wrong place. Instead of unpicking it, it is usually possible to overstitch in the correct colour. If there are several wrong stitches, it is better to unpick. On the right side, lift one of the offending stitches with a tapestry needle, and snip carefully using small pointed scissors. Unpick all the wrong stitches, then stitch in the ends on the back. Use a new length of yarn to re-stitch the missing stitches.

WORKING FROM A CHART

The designs in this book are all worked from colour charts. Although it may appear daunting to begin stitching on a large piece of blank canvas, it is easier than it looks. Each colour block on the chart represents a single tent stitch on the canvas. Because each stitch is worked over a thread of canvas, count the threads rather than the holes.

The colour charts have been generated on a special computer program and the printed colour blocks are as close a match as possible to the yarn colours. In some cases, where two shades of yarn are quite close, a symbol has been added to make the chart easy to follow. The key beside each chart shows exactly which colour block represents which colour.

Stitching diagonal lines

The main difficulty people have with needlepoint is working out how to stitch diagonal lines. On the chart, all the diagonal lines are the same but, when they are stitched they look different. In one direction (bottom left to top right) the stitches form a solid line, whereas in the other direction (top left to bottom right) the line is represented by a series of single parallel stitches.

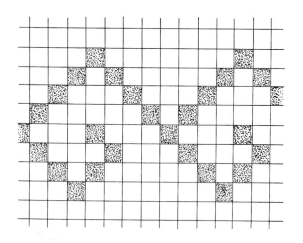

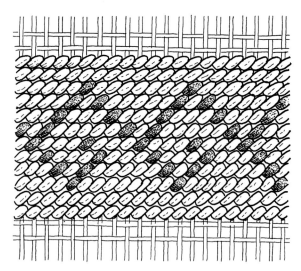

Working from split charts

Many of the needlepoint designs in this book are quite large, so their charts will not fit on a single page. You may find it helps to copy the pages on a colour photocopier, and piece the chart together before beginning. In this way, you can add notes and marks, indicating where you have stitched. If necessary, the charts can also be enlarged at the same time.

To piece a photocopied chart together, carefully trim down the edge of the colour blocks on each

section of the chart. Cut a piece of sticky tape the length of the trimmed edge and lay it, sticky side up, on a flat surface. Place one section halfway over the tape and carefully position the adjoining section of chart on the other half of the tape, so that the pattern and the grid lines match. Refer to the position and layout of the chart in the book. The top of the chart is always at the top of the book. Mark the top clearly on your new chart before beginning.

Working a repeat

Where a chart shows part of the design only, it is completed by repeating all or some of the chart. When this is necessary, each project has precise instructions explaining where to repeat. Borders and linear designs are completed by repeating the section of the design between marked lines. For example, the tiebacks on page 76 have shaped ends, with a central section that can be repeated two or three times, depending on the size of tieback required.

Square or rectangular projects are repeated by rotating the chart 180 degrees. Match the centre marks so that you do not stitch an extra row in the centre, and continue stitching until the design is complete.

STRETCHING THE FINISHED NEEDLEPOINT

Most needlepoint designs require stretching before being made up. When a design is worked entirely in tent stitch, the canvas inevitably becomes distorted, even if it has been worked on a frame. The stretching process also evens out the stitches, giving a more professional appearance. Do not trim the excess canvas from round the design until it has been stretched. Canvas is stretched by fixing it with drawing pins or carpet tacks to a drawing board, or piece of soft wood.

1 Cover the board with a piece of white fabric, and lay the needlepoint face down. Spray the back of the needlepoint with water until it is damp, but not wet.
2 Align one edge of the canvas with the top of the board. Beginning at one side, hammer tacks into the canvas, at intervals of 1–2·5cm ($1/2$–1in). Stretch the canvas slightly as you work, keeping the edge straight.

3 Pull the second side into shape, making sure that the corner with the first forms a right angle, and secure with tacks as before. Repeat the process along the other two sides. Double check that the corners are square and that the sides are straight.

4 Leave the stretched needlepoint to dry, away from direct heat. This should take about twenty-four hours, but could take longer. If the needlepoint was badly distorted, you may need to repeat the stretching, to ensure the corners are square.

Alternatively, the needlepoint can be steamed and pulled into a better shape before stretching. Pin the needlepoint loosely, face down, onto the board. Stand the board upright and aim the steam from a kettle or iron towards the canvas, taking care not to allow the iron to touch the yarn. Allow the needle-point to cool slightly, then pull into shape and stretch as above.

Some people advocate the use of wallpaper paste to help the needlepoint retain its shape after stretching. Many canvases already have size (a type of glue) added during manufacture, in which case, additional glue is unnecessary. It is also not necessary if the needlepoint is to be used for upholstery. If you do want to add wallpaper paste, stretch the needlepoint as before, then brush the ready-made paste over the back of the needlepoint while it is still tacked down. Allow to dry completely before removing the tacks.

JOINING TWO PIECES OF NEEDLEPOINT

If your design is too large to fit on your frame, or if you have made a mistake in measuring, and run out of canvas, you will need to join two pieces of canvas.

1 Work the needlepoint, leaving a single row unstitched on one edge, so that it can be used to cover the seam. Stretch both pieces of needlepoint and trim the canvas to 1cm (¹/₂ in).
2 Pin the two pieces together and machine stitch or backstitch down the row of canvas holes next to the last row of tent stitch. Open out the seam, and, using colours specified on the chart, complete the final row of needlepoint.

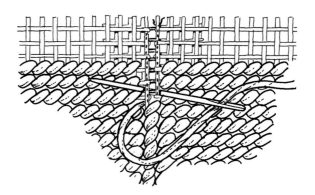

FABRICS FOR LINING AND BACKING

Needlepoint is a time consuming, but most rewarding, pastime so each stitched design warrants being finished to a high standard, using good-quality fabric. Most of the projects in this book require fabric to be applied to the needlepoint, either as a backing, or as a decorative feature. Any fabrics you use with tapestry canvas must be of a sufficient weight to support the heavy needlepoint, and must be suitable for dry cleaning. Furnishing fabrics such as velvet, and the more unusual, Indian, cotton fabrics, are ideal. Choose a fabric that enhances the design but does not overpower the needlepoint. If in doubt, match the fabric to the background colour. Backing fabrics can be a lighter weight, but they should be fairly closely woven. Natural fibres such as cotton or linen are best for backing.

JOINING FABRIC TO CANVAS

Wallhangings and rugs require a backing fabric to neaten the edges and protect the needlepoint from dust and dirt. The fabric can be stitched by machine, or by hand using back stitch.

1 Once the needlepoint has been stretched (see pages 116–17), trim the excess canvas to 1·5cm (⁵⁄₈in). Cut a piece of fabric the same size as the trimmed needlepoint, and pin the two together, right sides facing. Tack round the edge through both layers.

2 Whether using hand or machine, work with the canvas facing up, and sew along the edge of the last row of tent stitch, inserting the needle into every hole. If using a machine, position the zipper foot on the left side of a size 80 or 90 needle, and sew at low speed. Alter the stitch length so that the needle goes into every hole in the canvas. The zipper foot will hold the needlepoint in place and enable you to see where to stitch.

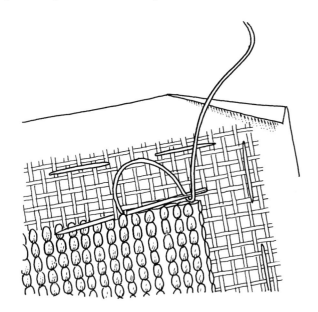

FRAMING NEEDLEPOINT WITH FABRIC

Small needlepoint designs can be framed with fabric to make a hanging or a large cushion cover. The matching camel and peacock designs on page 81 and page 84 are only 30cm (12in) square, but they have been made up into 45cm (18in) cushions by adding an 8cm (3in) border.

1 To make this width of border, cut four 11cm (4¼in) strips of fabric the length of the finished cushion plus 3cm (1¼in). Join the strips diagonally at each corner, leaving the inside seam allowance unstitched.

2 Press the seams open, and lay the fabric pieces right sides up, on top of the needlepoint. Turn back one inner seam at a time, then pin and tack the seam allowance along the edge of the needlepoint. Stitch close to the edge of the tent stitch. Press the framed panel on the right side, under a muslin cloth.

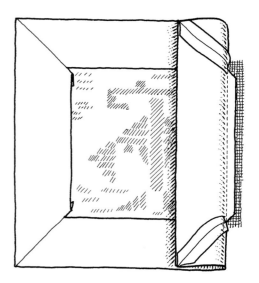

MAKING A CUSHION COVER

One of the simplest and most practical ways of making a cushion cover is by using an envelope opening, which has two pieces of overlapping fabric through which to insert the cushion pad. Piping can be applied at the end of step 1, before the backing is pinned in place.

1 Trim the excess canvas to 1·5cm (⁵⁄₈in). Cut a piece of fabric the same width as the canvas, and the length of the canvas plus 20cm (6in). Make a 1·5cm (⁵⁄₈in) hem along both short edges of the fabric and cut it in half lengthways.

2 With right sides facing, pin one cut edge to the left-hand side of the canvas and the other cut edge to the right-hand edge of the canvas. Overlap the two fabric panels and tack through all layers round the edge of the needlepoint.

3 Machine stitch all the way round the edge of the needlepoint close to the stitching. Trim the canvas to 1cm (¹/₂in) and the fabric to 1·5cm (⁵/₈in). Trim across the corners to reduce bulk and turn the cover right sides out.

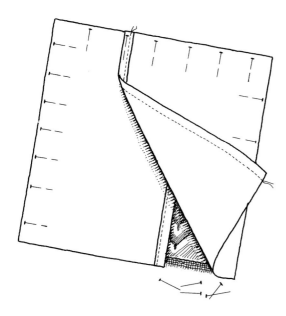

PIPING AND CORD EDGING
....

Cushion covers can be finished attractively with a cord or piped edging. Cord is hand-stitched round the finished cushion cover. Remember to wrap a short length of sticky tape round the cord before cutting, to prevent the cord unravelling. Unpick a few stitches at the bottom of the cushion cover and tuck one end of the cord inside. Using strong thread, stitch the cord to the edge of the cushion cover, all round, taking care not to pull the stitches too tight. Tuck the other end of the cord into the gap once you have stitched all the way round, and close the gap by stitching across it securely.

Cord can be difficult to attach securely, so it is now available with a flange (webbing strip) to make it easier to use. Flanged cord is attached to the cushion in the same way as piping. Piping cord can be bought in various thicknesses and is covered using bias strips of fabric. An attractive satin bias binding can be bought ready-made but it is easy to make your own from a matching fabric. You will need a piece of fabric about 45cm (18in) square to make the bias strips for a cushion.

Making bias strips
1 Trim the fabric along a thread, parallel to one of the edges. Fold the corner over at 45 degrees, until the cut edge is aligned along a thread. Crease or press the fold.
2 Open out the fabric. Use tailor's chalk and a ruler to mark parallel lines 6cm (2¹/₂in) apart. Cut the fabric into strips and press to remove some of the stretch.

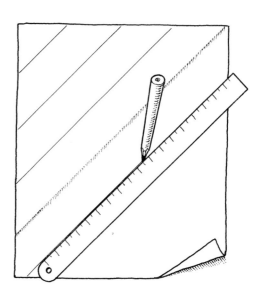

3 Overlap the strips, as shown, right sides facing. Pin and stitch where the edges cross over. Press the seam open and trim off the little triangles to align the fabric.

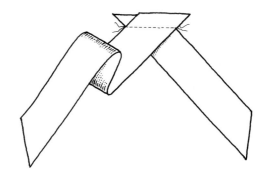

Piping
1 Make a bias strip long enough to fit round the edge of the cushion cover, including a 5cm (2in) allowance. Cut a piece of piping cord the same length. Fold the fabric round the piping cord, right side facing out, and tack.

2 Beginning in the centre of the bottom edge of the cushion cover, pin the piping round the edge, on the right side of the canvas, matching the raw edges. Before tacking, trim the ends of the piping cord to different lengths. Join the bias strip using a diagonal seam as before, overlap the trimmed piping cord, and pin in place.

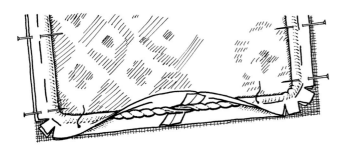

3 Tack close to the piping cord. Pin the cushion cover back and front together, right sides facing. Tack and stitch as described on page 118.

MITRING A CORNER
....

Mitring corners reduces unnecessary bulk and produces a neat corner when applying a fabric backing to the needlepoint.

1 Fold the hem carefully and press in position. Open out the hem and fold the corner over.

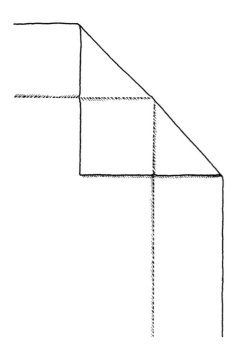

2 Press along the fold, open out and trim to 5mm (¼in). Fold the hem again along the pressed lines to form a neat mitred corner.

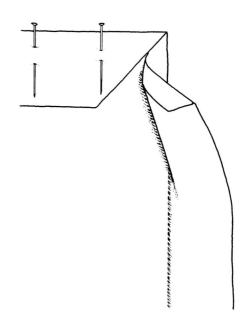

HANGING METHODS
....

Velcro and batten

1 Cut a length of Velcro slightly narrower than the wallhanging. Stitch one piece of the Velcro along the top edge of the backing fabric, before attaching the backing fabric to the wallhanging.

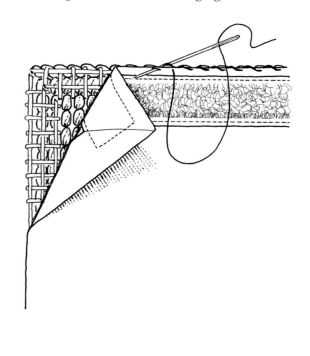

2 Cut a wooden batten slightly narrower than the wallhanging, and fix it to a wall. Nail the other piece of the Velcro to the top edge of the batten, and fasten the wallhanging in place.

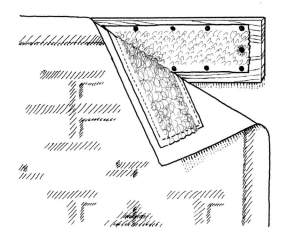

Dowel and casing

1 Unpick a few stitches at the top of each side of the wallhanging, and insert a dowel between the canvas and the backing fabric.
2 Decorate the dowel ends with tassels and hang the dowel from an attractive cord.

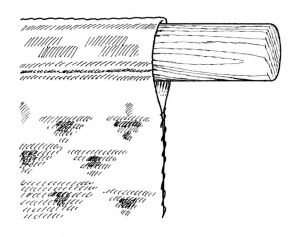

Dowel and fringe

1 Attach a long fringe, at least 15cm (6in), to the top edge of the needlepoint. Plait the fringe and finish the ends with small tassels or beads (see pages 123–4).

2 Tie the decorated plaits round a dowel, and hang the dowel from an attractive cord.

ADDITIONAL DECORATIONS

Kilims are often finished with fringes, tassels, beads or shells. The addition of ornaments adds to the entire design, improving its quality, durability and appearance. Kilims made for weddings and religious ceremonies are particularly lavishly adorned, as are those used on camels and horses. Some decorations, such as blue glass beads, are added to ward off evil spirits, or as a symbol of good luck.

In our needlepoint projects, fringes and tassels can be optional, so the quantities of wool required to make them have not been included in the project instructions. Once the needlepoint is stitched, you may have sufficient left to complete the fringe or tassels.

Making a fringe

Kilim fringes are made by tying the warp threads when the kilim is removed from the loom. Needlepoint canvas does not have warp threads, but a fringe can be attached to the final row of canvas holes, once the project has been made up.

1 Cut bundles of yarn 2½–3 times the intended length of the fringe. Thread the two cut ends from one length into a tapestry needle. If using crewel wool, work with several lengths together.
2 Working from the right side, take the needle through a hole in the canvas in the last row of tent stitches, then through the loop at the other end of the yarn, and pull tight.

Continue along the edge of the needlepoint until the fringe is complete. When adding a fringe to 10-, 12- or 14-count canvas, it is sufficient to loop a length of yarn through every second hole.

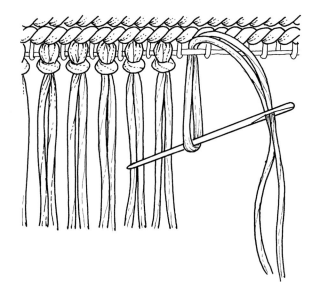

Knotted fringe
Group the fringe threads into equal bundles. Tie each bundle with an overhand knot positioned close to the edge of the needlepoint. Trim the ends neatly.

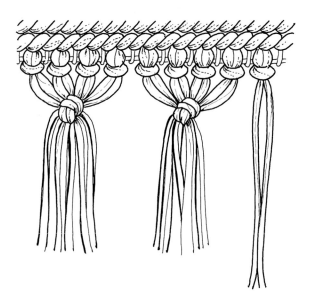

Net fringe
Knot together adjacent pairs of fringe threads. Separate the resulting bundles into two, and knot them with the adjacent bundles, as shown in the diagram. Continue until the net fringe is as deep as required.

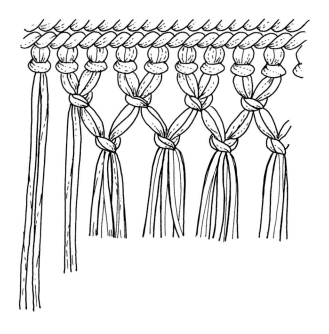

Braided fringe
Group the fringe ends together in multiples of three. Plait the bundles and wrap the ends with a contrasting colour. Two or three plaits can be wrapped together for a different effect (see page 123).

Making a cord
A wide selection of ready-made cords is available, but you could make your own quite easily, by plaiting or twisting. Tapestry wool and crewel wool are suitable for making cords, as are embroidery thread and crochet cotton. Colours and yarns can be mixed together to produce unusual effects.

Twisted cord
1 Cut enough lengths of yarn, at least double the finished length of the cord, to make a bundle about half as thick as the required cord. Tie one end of the bundle to something solid, such as a door handle, and tie the other end round a pencil.

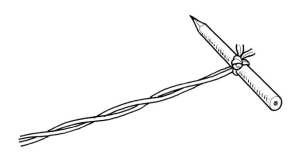

2 Keeping the yarn bundle fairly taut, turn the pencil clockwise until the cord is twisted tightly. Take hold of the middle of the cord and, keeping the cord taut, bring the two ends together. Let go of the middle, to allow the cord to twist up. Tie the two ends together, then hit the edge of a table with the finished cord, to even out the twists.

Plaited cord

1 Fasten three bundles of yarn together at one end. Pin to a board, or tie on to a solid object such as a door handle. Cross the left bundle over the centre bundle and then the right bundle over the new centre bundle.

2 Repeat until the desired length is reached. Secure the ends by tying a knot or wrapping (see right).

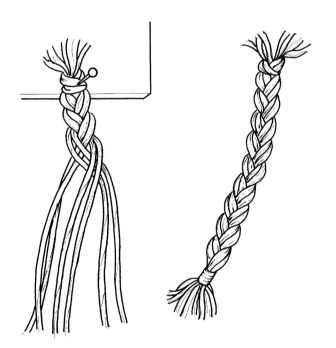

Wrapping

Wrapping is an effective and decorative way of tying a bundle of threads or a plaited cord, and of finishing tassels, or attaching tassels to cords or fringes. The instructions below describe finishing a tassel but, they could be adapted for any situation.

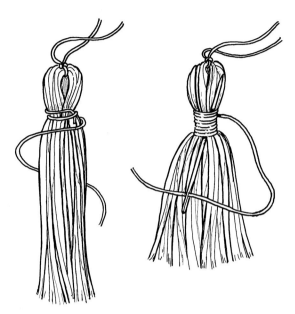

1 Lay the thread along the section of tassel you want to wrap. Holding the thread firmly with your finger, begin to wrap the thread round the tassel, trapping the end of the thread under the wrapping.

2 Lay each successive thread carefully next to the previous one. Keep the thread taut, and continue wrapping until the required depth is reached. Thread the end into a tapestry needle and take it under the wrapping. Pull tight and trim.

Tassels

Tassels form an essential part of some kilim designs. Small tassels added to the edge of Qashqai kilims are a symbol of good luck, and three special tassels hanging from salt bags are said to protect the valuable contents. Tassels decorated with cowrie shells and beads, or wrapped with luxurious gold thread, can transform a simple kilim. There are two basic tassels which can be adapted to make larger more ornate tassels for the corners of cushions. It is also quite easy to customize bought tassels so that they co-ordinate with your needlepoint.

Tassel 1

1 Cut a piece of card about 8cm (3in) long, slightly longer than the finished length of the tassel. Wrap the yarn round the card until the required thickness is reached.

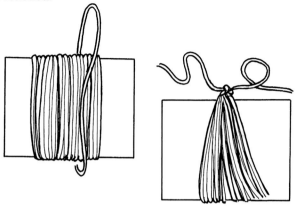

2 Using a tapestry needle, thread a double length of yarn under the yarn at one end of the card and tie. Cut the yarn along the opposite edge. Make a 'neck' on the tassel using the wrapping technique.

Tassel 2

This tassel looks very professional, as it is attached to a cord or plait.

1 Cut a piece of card about 8cm (3in) long, slightly longer than the finished length of the tassel. Wrap the yarn round the card until the required thickness is reached.

2 Cut along one edge of the card. Put a length of strong thread on a flat surface and lay the bundle of yarn across it. Tie a knot in the end of a cord or plaited cord, and place on top of the yarn, with the knot just below the strong thread.

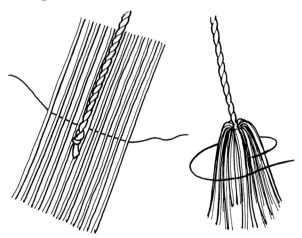

3 Tie the length of thread around the yarn and the cord, above the knot. Ease the yarn round, to cover all sides of the cord. Hold the end of the cord so that the yarn falls down over the knot to form the tassel. Wrap some yarn below the knot to form a 'neck' and complete the tassel.

Customizing tassels

Plain tassels can be wrapped with contrasting yarns to match the needlepoint. Bullions, which are short lengths of handmade cord, can be stitched round the head of the tassel to add a luxurious touch. Beads may be sewn in a ring round the 'neck' or threaded onto the 'skirt' of the tassel and secured with a knot. Bundles of small tassels can be tied together and fixed to a cord by wrapping. The possibilities are as great as your imagination. Use beads, shells and different yarns to make exquisite tassels that will make each project unique.

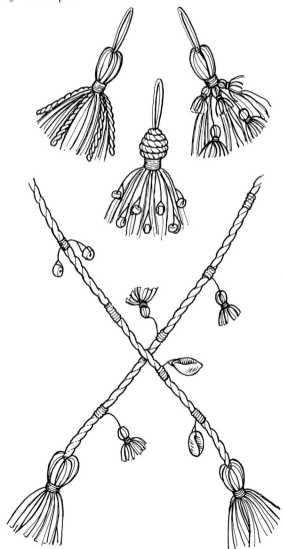

The yarns used in this book are mainly Anchor tapestry wool and Appleton crewel wool. Anchor is sold world-wide but Appleton may not be so readily available. Appleton crewel wools were selected because of the wide colour range available, but DMC Médici's crewel wool can be used instead.

This conversion chart gives the nearest equivalent colour of DMC Médici's crewel wool to those used from Appleton's range. The colour match is quite close but not exact, so it is advisable to use the specified brand of yarn if possible. If you choose to use an alternative yarn, use that type for the whole project rather than mixing two different brands.

Conversion charts between Anchor and DMC colours are readily available from your local needlecraft shop.

Appleton Crewel Wool	DMC Médici's Crewel Wool	Appleton Crewel Wool	DMC Médici's Crewel Wool
121	8118	504	8102
125	8107	505	8100
126	8221	692	8327
151	8214	701	8842
153	8202	841	8328
155	8203	843	8304
205	8107	862	8173
207	8221	865	8129
209	8100	866	8128
321	8932	882	8502
323	8931	922	8932
325	8202	924	8930
326	8201	926	8205
327	8205	961	8380
328	8200	964	8204
331a	8421	967	8500
333	8400	983	8308
358	8417	988	8512
471	8326	992	ecru
473	8325	993	noir
503	8103	998	8713

Acknowledgements

I would like to thank the many people who helped with this publication. The book would not have been possible but for the long hours devoted to stitching the designs. Special thanks go to Jenny Blair, Linda Fraser, Lis Gunner, Claire Metson, Brenda Sandford-Monk, Barbara Smith, Adelle Wainwright, Hayley Wainwright and Rita Watson.

Particular thanks are due to the Editorial and Design teams at Cassell, in particular, Helen Denholm, Zoë Hughes, Rosie Anderson and Caroline Hyams. Thanks also to Vivienne Wells for her input on the text, Ethan Danielson for the charts, Gail Engert for the attractive book design and Ed Barber for the excellent photography.

Thanks also to Julie Gill and Sally Jefferson at Coats Craft, Peter Armitage at Appleton Wools and Cara Ackerman at DMC for their help in supplying the materials for the projects.

The yarns and canvases used in the projects should be available from your local needlecraft shop. If there are any problems please contact the following companies who will be pleased to help:

canvas and tapestry wool: Coats Craft UK, Darlington (01325 365457)

crewel and tapestry wool: Appleton Brothers, London (0181 994 0711)

coton perlé: DMC Creative World, Leicestershire (0116 281 1040).

Pronunciation Guide

Jose Luczyc-Wyhowska of The Kilim Warehouse has kindly helped the publishers in compiling the following list of words that might cause difficulties in pronunciation:

abrash	arbrash
Afyon	Afion
Aimaq	Eyemac
çengel	chengel
çiçims	gigims
çuval	chuwal
göz	gerse
gül	ghoul
haç	hatch
Keçimuhsine	Ketchimusneigh
Kharaqai	Karakeye
Khorasan	Horassan
koçboynuzu	kurtchboysnou
Manastir	Manaster
Moghan	Mohan
Mukkur	Mudjur
Qashqai	Cashkiee
Taimani Aimaq	Tiemani Eyemac
Yüncü	Yunjew
Yüncü Yörük	Yunjew Yuruk

Index